KARMA, The Bewildered Witch

Vipul Barpute

Invincible Publishers

First published in India in 2017 by Invincible Publishers

ISBN: 978-93-86148-35-3

Invincible Publishers
F-55, Sushant Lok II, Hong Kong Bazar Lane Sector 57, Gurgaon-122003

Opposite Kasturba Ashram, Radaur Distt Yamuna Nagar, Haryana- 135133

DEDICATION

This book,
the very 1st book of mine
is dedicated to my love, whom
I promised to be with her
till my last breath
and
all my family members
specially to my beloved friends

Acknowledgment

* * *

We would like to thank our beloved brother Vipul for such a wonderful story and also for the memories he spent with us. We would also like to thank both Uncle and Aunty for supporting and encouraging us throughout the journey and also extends our thanks to all the people who supported us throughout our journey and especially those who didn't support us, it was because of them we gained more confidence and started to believe in ourselves.

Big thanks to Invincible Publishers, who believed in us and always, guided us till the end. It is because of them, that we could finally bring out the story of our beloved brother. We would also thank Ms. Sneha Agarwal for such a wonderful cover page and all the work. Big thanks to Mr. Ajay Setia and his team for believing in us and letting our dream come true.

We would also like to thank each and every one who helped, supported and guided us throughout our journey.

Prologue

* * *

There have been many ups and downs, but the only thing that remains constant is the memories. Everything is fixed; finally both the couples are getting hitched. It's a beautiful evening; the arrangements have been made. The people are overwhelmed at seeing the bride.

Everyone is waiting for the groom to arrive, but where is the groom is the question that arises, as the time flies the question gets deeper and deeper. Did he run away? Is he in some kind of trouble?

Karma answers all your questions. Read on to know the story...

THE UNIVERSAL LAW OF KARMA

Nothing happens by chance or outside the Universal laws. Every action has a reaction or consequence and as the saying goes "As you sow, so you reap".

Time and circumstances can change at any time.

Don't devalue or hurt anyone in life.

You may be powerful today. But remember, Time is more powerful than you!

Chapter 1: The Introduction

* * *

It was a winter season and it's impossible to wake up from the warmth of the blanket and go to school, since I was in the 9th standard my pre-finals were nearing so; I had to take up the challenge of getting up and heading to the school. As usual, I woke up; brushing my teeth I looked at myself in the mirror and continued. At a point when I opened my mouth there were bubbles coming out of the mouth, I was unable to speak due to the continuous flow of bubbles from the mouth, so I started screaming, calling out names but everything went in vain. I thought that I had become dumb and gave up. Later, when I rinsed my mouth, the voice was back. I looked around and to my shock; I found out that I had put the shampoo on my toothbrush instead of the toothpaste which caused the bubbles to flow out of the mouth. Finally, I was relieved to have my voice back.

As soon as I had my breakfast, I left. Putting on the ear pods and taking the cycle I headed towards school. The weather was too cold outside with dry leaves covering the road, the street lights were on, dew which was formed on the leaves made the leaves come back to life, and only a few people dared to face such a cold breeze and I was one among them. The people were rushing to tea stalls to keep themselves warm over a cup of tea. I too thought of putting up a tea stall which would help me earn enough to get myself a scooty, but suddenly the thought went off the mind when my favorite song started playing "*Sunn raha hai na tu*", it was a hit song way back that time. I was busy humming that song and suddenly something happened that made my mind go blank, when I got back to my senses, I was on the ground with the bicycle beside me on the left side and a beautiful girl on the right side. I just looked up and thanked God for giving me such a beautiful morning.

I got up and helped her, she refused my help at first, but when she couldn't help herself it was my turn to help her. That was the first time when her hand went into my hand. Who knew what was written in my destiny. She was scolding me for not responding to her bell, I seriously didn't even hear a single word and was just staring at her beautified face. My eyes were not able to move away from staring at her lips even for a second, when she finally zoomed away with her bicycle, I got back to my senses and then picking up the damaged bicycle I headed to school.

I reached school on time, parked my bicycle and ran to the school ground. The national anthem was about to begin, I stood in my class line and after singing the national anthem the principal came around to check everyone's uniform. When he came to me he looked at my face, it was full of dust and my school uniform was torn from here and there, just don't ask where it wasn't, such was the condition. The most important thing was that I was bleeding from hand to toe still I didn't have any sensation.

Later, I went to the medication room where I bandaged my bleeding arm and leg. I was in no pain as the face of that beautiful girl whom I had come across earlier in the morning was flashing in front of me. It was like love at first sight kind of thing. The bell rang and I rushed to my classroom.

It was the science hour, again the same chemicals, acids and all. It was such a boring period and the lecturer too was an old aged man. His name was Mr. Chatterjee, a Bengali who daily ate hilsa fish; it's a fact that if you don't eat hilsa fish then you are not a Bengali. I always topped his subject and he used to be envious of my marks as he always expected his daughter who was in the same class to top his subject.

Since it was a chilly morning the view from the window was stunning. Especially the dried leaves on the ground, which gave more beauty to the road, the street-lights on, made people feel that it was still night, the rush at the tea stall helped people feel better from the bitter cold. I was completely mesmerized by the beauty of the nature. I didn't hear Mr. Chatterjee calling out my roll number. I came back to my senses only when Mr. Chaterjee hurled a chalk piece towards me and told me to answer his question. The question was "*What is the molecular formula of urea*" and instead of answering the molecular formula I answered "*yellow*", the whole class started laughing and at that time Mr. Chatterjee's face turned to the color of red tomatoes. I could easily notice that his blood pressure might have shot up to 350. Before he could tell me the next thing, I just took my book and ran out of the class. I could sense a sigh of relief on his face.

I knew that once I get out of the class, my dearest friend Akash would also accompany me and as expected, he too was soon thrown out of the class. We celebrated by going to the canteen, it was the daily procedure of us getting thrown out of Mr. Chatterjee's class. It was too much fun and since it was bitter cold outside, we opted for something hot like French fries and a Frankie.

I know that your readers might be thinking how we used to get all these in the school canteen. Ours was an international school, so we were lucky enough to get all these things but only seasonal wise. After having the hot foodies it was time to get back to the class. We then rushed back to the class as Mr. Chatterjee's class was about to end.

When the bell rang it was time for encounter between Mr. Chatterjee's and us. After taking attendance, he came outside and everyone gathered, I mean all the three sections were looking out from the class window, some of them even gathered at the corridors to notice the fierce encounter between us. As usual the Mr. Chatterjee started "*See you both belong to an international school, your parents are toiling hard day and night for your future and how are you paying back to them, is it in this way?*" Starting it looked realistic, but later I came to know he was keeping me out of the class in order to secure a place for his daughter. So each and every word he said we used to just nod our heads and laugh looking at each other.

This would anger him and then he would scold us in some unknown language. This daily encounter lasted for about 10 min and now it had become a common thing. The next hour was of Mrs. Sharada, she was our mathematics lecturer who knew of all this drama and always supported us.

We went back to our bench and sat there. I was busy looking and admiring the beautiful nature, when

I suddenly heard some soothing voice near my ears. It gave a soft feeling as if some angel had got down to earth only for my sake. When I turned I was like '*you?*' and from the other side, she too was astonished seeing me and the same word was called from her mouth '*you?*' Everyone looked at us with a doubt on their face. The Ma'am from other end said "*what are you people doing 'you'*". Ms. Sharada introduced the so called "*you*" as Sivangi, our new classmate.

I could see everyone was looking at me as if I had committed some crime by telling '*you*'. Akash too was puzzled as how did I know her and why did I say '*you*', everyone had the same doubt in their mind. The lecturer called the new student '*you*' I mean Sivangi upon the dice and asked to briefly introduce herself.

She told about herself, her parents and about the previous school and everything blah blah. The only thing that caught my attention was when she had spoken about her encounter with me early this morning. The words she said was, "*I met a student of this class early today morning when I was heading towards my new school as everyone are excited to explore their new schools I too was, but someone from this class ignored my bell and was just listening to his favorite song, he was so much into the song, that he hit me and this is why I had got late on my first day. But, yes, there is one thing about that person he is helpful and caring*".

By this till now I guess you might have also understood whom she was referring to. Yes, exactly the people of my class too understood and they started staring at me as if I had stolen their food.

Akash couldn't stop staring at me with blood red color in his eyes. I could sense that I would become their food for the day as everyone was ready to prowl upon me with a hunch bunch of questions. I nodded which meant I would answer all their questions which saved me for the day.

After the brief, not exactly brief but life threatening introduction the lecturer told her to get back to her seat and what yes she had chosen to sit beside me. She could sense I was angry and the best thing I love about girls is they know how to easily divert the topic and yes they are aware of our weaknesses.

She came to me and stated, "*Hey Hi, I am Sivangi nice to meet you*", to which I replied "*I already know it!*" I avoided her for some time and she too ignored as if there was no one sitting beside her. After a while she looked at me and said "*Are you still not going to talk to me?*" To which I replied "*I guess so*" the next thing was like a warning to me, she said "*Ok, so I'm going and sitting beside someone else, goodbye*" after saying this which boy would want such a beautiful girl to go and sit beside someone else, so I replied "*Ok, I am ready to talk to you*".

Chapter 2: Friendship Is Born

* * *

Days went on, and none of us spoke. Classes were in full swing and each one of us was busy with the projects. Then, the following day she came up to me said "*Are you seriously not going to talk to me?*", but before I could answer her first question, the second question was fired at me "*Are we going to be like strangers*", then I understood if I didn't stop her, a series of questions would be fired at me at an unstoppable rate. So, before she could ask anything else I just placed a finger on her lips. This was the first time I was touching some girl's lip and I thanked my stars that I just did it with my fingers not something else. I guess you all might have understood what '*not something else means*'. What do you think would I get a chance of touching her lips with something else? Let's see if destiny had that plan for me.

So I started to answer her questions "*See we are friends and yes we will not remain strangers for sure, I guarantee u that*", I guess she was relieved by my answer. Later on it was the recess hour, so three of us ran to the canteen as we were very hungry after all those project works.

Akash, Sivangi and I made a good gang. We always cracked jokes and the best part was that we laughed on our own jokes. I used to go to Sivangi's apartment daily and from there we used to head to our school. The motive behind that was I could spend some quality time with her.

She started telling about her previous school, her friends and how she was bullied in her previous school. We told about our school and other activities that took place in the school. The only difference between us was she always used to top the class and I used to be the topper but from the bottom. We always used to secure our places, one from the top and the other from the bottom.

Later on I came to know that her father was in the military. It's very difficult to have a friend whose father is in the military, those strict rules and all makes me go mad. For now, her dad was posted in Jammu and Kashmir. She always used to miss her dad. One day, she invited Akash and Me for dinner. That day I met her mom, there house was like one big palace decorated with many artifacts. There were also various collections of guns hung on the walls. I thought to myself if I take our relation ahead of friendship, then her dad would shoot me with each and every gun hung up there. I thought that being shot by shotgun would be better and smiled at my own thought.

There she was; her mom dressed in the beautiful Indian attire. We complimented her mom for her sari, she was blushing. I guess uncle rarely admired her. Sivangi went in to change her dress till then we chit-chatted with aunty. We told her about the city, the places that can be visited and about our school. She showed us the medals Sivangi received in her previous school. Not even in a single picture did I notice her dad being beside her while receiving the award except for a family vacation photo.

Here came the most beautiful girl on the planet, Sivangi. She was dressed in her blue top with black denim jeans. She was looking damn hot in her outfit, the temperature around me just shot up and my mouth was wide open. Akash noticed this and told me shut my mouth; he did so by pinching me on my thighs such an asshole he was.

We then handed over the bouquet to aunty and a pack of chocolates to Sivangi, both of them blushed and then it was time for dinner. I was a big foodie those days. When aunt opened the top of the lid, the smell was making me go mad. I couldn't wait anymore as I was starving since morning. I told mom not to make breakfast as I had planned to keep my tummy empty for the sumptuous dinner. Aunty had made my favorite curry Malai-Kofta. She served all of us and I ate till my tummy was full. When I couldn't eat anymore, I gave up. Later, we had ice-cream and talked about school and the upcoming exams.

It was almost 10:00 pm when we had the last scoop of ice-cream. We had to rush back home as it was already late. So we bid goodbye and thanked aunty and Sivangi for such a sumptuous meal and left.

We were now busy with our upcoming exams the dangerous one's the half yearly exams. Mr. Chaterjee had already been preparing to fail me this time as he had faith that his daughter would top his subject, but I too didn't want to let him down by failing in his subject.

We started studying day and night since each one wanted to top the class. It was like we all were bulls left in the race and only one could survive i.e. top the class.

Finally, the half yearly exams started and in no time we were in the middle of our exams. There was a surprise waiting at the end of our exams. Wait, you too will come to know about the surprise once the exams end.

We had gone through the deadliest phase of our life, the exams. Each one of us was relieved once the last paper ended. Rather than discussing how the exam went we were thinking of the surprise. Everyone was told to attend a meeting which would take place in the auditorium the next day.

We three too thought what it might be. I was happy if Mr. Chatterjee would leave the school tomorrow as he had already grown too old for us. We were eager for the next day as everyone was told to dress in their casuals rather than school uniforms.

Finally the next day, arrived the sun shone bright and we reached school in much advance. Our principal Ms. Megha had arrived and all of us were instructed to be seated down in the auditorium and wait for the announcement.

The principal arrived and everyone wished her. For the first half and hour the topic was how each one of us had written the exam. Then came a surprise to all of us. Our school had planned an excursion to the 9th and 10th standard students. We all were excited as this time we were given an opportunity of visiting South India.

The date was fixed and each one of us was given itinerary about day to day plan and places to be covered during the 10 day trip. The only problem was getting permission from our parents.

We went home and decided to talk to our parents. My dad readily agreed, but mom's being themselves couldn't as she was afraid of sending me alone. I had to explain mom in detail about each and every thing which took time but later she too agreed. Now, it was we who had to convince Sivangi's mom. First she was not ready to send her, but later we told aunty that we all are there to take care of her and especially me. When I said "Aunty, don't worry, I am there to take care of your Barbie", I could see Sivangi blush. Aunty too agreed to a condition that I take proper care of her.

Now what, it was fun time, packing time and we all were busy but not me. I was busy writing this to keep my readers updated about each and everything.

Chapter 3: Is It Love Or Attraction?

* * *

Finally Dasara holidays began and we too were prepared to leave Hyderabad. Dad and uncle had come to drop me at the station. Sivangi and her mom had also come to the station. My eyes couldn't stop staring her as she was looking much beautiful than the morning. She had worn blue t-shirt with black denim jeans. I was like a statue for about 10-15 min. My mind went blank and I guess she had noticed me staring at her. She came to me and asked "*Do I look that hot, that people forget that their parents too are around*". I was like "*Hey, your dress is so beautiful, you look stunning in this*", saying this I then went to aunty and started speaking to her.

The train was to depart at around 10:00 AM in the morning. So, we were given instructions to look for our respective seats and settle. Boys and girls were given seats in different compartment and a lecturer in each compartment and as expected the lecturer in our compartment was none other than my old-age enemy Mr. Chaterjee.

Mr. Chatterjee was given the seat beside me. Everyone expected a world war 3 between us. His daughter too accompanied him for the South Tour. She had worn an Indian outfit and was looking stunning. I complimented her for her look and from nowhere Mr. Chatterjee happened to come and everyone from our compartment and the girl's compartment gathered to watch a live war.

But nothing such happened, he calmly told me to get to my seat and told his daughter to go to the other compartment and find her seat. I knew Mr. Chatterjee's behavior. I thought how he let me go without even uttering a word.

Now it was time to leave Hyderabad. The train started moving and everyone, including me had tears in my eyes as it was the first time I was going away from my parents for a span of 10 days. The best part was Mr. Chatterjee's daughter too started to weep. When everyone asked her the reason she said "*My dad is coming with me, so I will be having restrictions*", listening to her, everyone had a hearty laugh.

Later I went to the girl's compartment to call Sivangi for antakshari. We all sang songs for our partners, but as destined, my partner was not Sivangi but the traditional dressed girl Megha. Yes, she was my partner and I could sense jealousy on Sivangi's face.

On the other end, I could sense anger on Mr. Chatterjee's face, from the corner of his eyes, he was staring me as if I would be his meal tonight. He had also skipped lunch I guess to keep his tummy empty, so that he could have me as his dinner.

Later, after everyone had a sumptuous dinner, went to sleep as we already had a tiring day and also needed to be afresh the following day. The lights were turned off and we all slept.

The next morning we got up at around 7:00

am, and by 8:30 we were served breakfast. After having breakfast we started packing our luggage as it was time for the Thiruvananthapuram station to arrive. It had been almost a 23 hour journey on the train. A station arrived whose name was similar to Thiruvananthapuram. Some friends, assuming it to be the Thiruvananthapuram station got down the train, I too got down with them and when we noticed the name of the station it was written Trichapally. By the time we could understand that it was not the right station, the train started and we panicked. All of us started running in the direction of the train; the speed of the train was catching up slowly and we ran like there was a marathon going on, never in my life had I run like this. Slowly, one by one got into the train except me and suddenly the train sped up, I threw my luggage and jumped inside the compartment. My legs were hurt, but thank god I got into the compartment safely.

All of us were relieved. Sivangi ran to me a slapped me on my cheek. I was shocked and everyone was stunned by this. She then cried and hugged me. Everyone present there hooted and clapped. Mr. Chatterjee came to me and he too slapped me and told me never to do such things in my life. I could see a tear in his eyes. This was the first time I saw Mr. Chatterjee in tears. I thanked god for my safety.

Now our actual station arrived. All of us were greeted with a red rose; a bus was arranged for our tour. We all sat with our partners, and I think by now you all might have got to know who my partner was; you all might be thinking it to be Sivangi, but no she wasn't my partner, it was none other than Mr. Chatterjee's daughter.

It was like we were missing each other and Mr. Chatterjee's daughter sensed that thing and she agreed to swap partners. Now we both were together and got some more time to spend with each other. We reached the hotel and everyone was allotted rooms with three boys in each room and same for the girls. We all had to assemble at around 4:00 pm at the center hall. As, we were tired we went to our respective rooms and freshened up. Later it was lunch time and the best part of the hotel was that there were ostriches all around the garden, all of us were served lunch in the garden so we had the ostriches moving around us. The girls were afraid of the ostriches so everyone held their partners hand. Sivangi too held my hand; I could feel the warmth of her hands as if she wanted to convey something to me.

After lunch everyone was instructed to get ready by 5:30 in the evening. We all assembled at the hotel lobby and everyone was instructed to get into the bus along with their partners and take their seats. Sivangi and I luckily got a window seat. The weather outside was a bit drizzly. Every vehicle had their headlamps on, which added more beauty to the street. The smell of the wet mud made of all us go mad, we were continuously breathing in for that smell.

Finally, we reached the fishing nets area where large nets were used to catch fishes. These nets were double the size of a giant. We were taken around to show how these nets are made. Mr. Chatterjee accidentally put his hand into one of the nets, then when his hand was stuck in that and I went to him and whispered in his ears "Sir, there is no way out, your hand needs to be cut to get out of this". He was tensed; it was the first time his face turned pale. We called a fisherman and he helped sir out of this and yes, that too, without cutting sir's hand. Everyone present there had a hearty laugh.

We were let off to stroll around the area. Sivangi, Sush, Akash and I were damn hungry, so we went to a stall and had chat. When our tummy didn't fill then we tried something special and awkward. We were given ice-cream in the cone and topped with different flavors of various scoops and an additional topping of tomato ketchup.

The taste was yummy, but the combination was awkward. Later, the port lights were switched on which made the port glitter. We all were instructed to get into the boat, and were taken around the sea where we got to see the Indian Navy Ships. Those ships were so large that it was impossible to see the whole ship from our small boat.

Later, at around 9:00pm we were taken back to our hotel. The evening was spent beautifully. Moreover, we were very hungry and the dinner was not yet ready. So, we planned to go to our rooms and get freshened up, later would go for dinner. We all went to our rooms and changed into casuals. I had worn my favorite white shirt and shorts and was waiting for Akash to get ready, but that asshole was in the washroom trying up all the combinations and when finally he was satisfied we locked the room and left.

A girl walked passed by me. I couldn't recognize her as I was busy texting my mom. But the fragrance reminded me of Sivangi. When, I turned and looked back she was long gone. I called her up to ask her where she was, she replied "*I just passed by you and gave you something*". I searched my pockets and everything but nothing was to be found. I asked her "*tell me what it is*", she said "*A million dollar smile and giggled*".

We later met at the dinner hall. She was dressed in her denim shorts and red top. She was looking stunning; I couldn't stop myself from staring at her. She was the beauty whom I had dreamt of. I asked myself "*Do, I love her, have I fallen for her*", these questions were arising in my mind.

I wasn't able to answer those questions arising in my mind. My mind was telling me it was just attraction, but the heart told me to tell her. I was smiling looking at her; she saw me and asked "*what*"? I nodded my head and kept on staring her.

Later, we were told to have our dinner. The dinner provided was sumptuous as we were provided with the best food available in Thiruvananthapuram.

After a sumptuous dinner, we strolled around the garden with hand in hand. There was a mini zoo, which had parrots, ostriches and other little animals. The weather outside was cool and she was feeling cold, luckily I had worn a blazer and when she rubbed her hands to her shoulders I could see that she was feeling cold. I put my blazer around her shoulders and in return she gave me a smile.

Later, all of us went to our respective room and dozed off to bed. The next morning we were to go to the famous temple in Kerala, the Padmanabhaswamy temple. We woke up at around 7:00 am and got ready by 8:30. We wore jeans and t-shirt and the girls were dressed in a golden light cream with yellow bordered saris. Everyone was looking stunning and this was the first time we saw our class girls wearing saris.

My eyes were searching for Sivangi, but she hadn't come down till now. I asked her friends to which they replied "*She's getting ready*", we waited and finally the princess put her foot steps on the ground. As usual, she was beautiful which made the day even more beautiful.

We all got into the bus and left for the temple. There was a surprise waiting only for the boys at the temple. When we got down the bus we boys were instructed to get into a room. None of us knew what that was. We got into the room and saw Mr. Chatterjee trying to wear a Lungi, a traditional dress. But his stomach was not allowing him to tie that Lungi.

We all were told to remove our shirts and pants as leather belts were prohibited inside the temple. So, we all wore banyan along with the Lungi. Mr.Chatterjee was not able to wear his Lungi. Finally, Mr. Chatterjee breathed in and tied up his Lungi.

We came out of the room and seeing us in this dress, the girls started giggling. I looked at Sivangi and asked her how it is; she gave a deep smile and nodded her head saying awesome.

There was a large door at the entrance of the temple; the door was made of wood which was strong enough. There were carvings all over the temple premises which described city of Kerala those days. There were carvings of gods and goddesses. The temple was full of positive energy, your mind gets relaxed and it takes you back to that era.

Then was the main entrance to the Padmanabhaswamy temple. There was a large idol of Lord Vishnu in a sleeping position. It is considered to be one of the wealthiest temples in the world. The idol was beautiful. We entered the temple premises took darshan and each one of us wished something. It is said that all your wishes would be fulfilled in the temple.

We then took prasad; the interesting thing about the prasad is that it is yummy and once you have that prasad you will feel your stomach heavy. Later, we were taken to those five vaults. Among those five vaults only three of them have been opened. When those three vaults were opened a large amount of treasure was discovered in it. But, the fourth vault among those was the most secretive vault which couldn't be opened till date. This remains a mystery as the vault is protected by a large iron door which contains neither locks nor any nuts or bolts.

It is said that the vault is protected by two large serpents and it contains some mysterious information about the universe and it can only be opened by chanting some powerful Vedic mantras. It is also said that the person who tries to break the vault either gets injured or dies. Every one of us was shocked after learning about this vault. Then we all were given some time to move around the temple and look at those beautified carvings.

Later, in the afternoon we left the temple and went to the hotel. It was lunch time and all of us were hungry. There were delicious meals served along with dessert. Our tummies were full and even were not able to walk.

Finally, seeing our conditions the principal had given us permission to take rest. We could somehow manage but Mr.Chatterjee had to take help of 3-4 waiters to get to the room. His stomach was about to burst. When we passed by Mr.Chaterjee we could smell some poisonous, unbreathable gases which came with some strange sounds. We couldn't bare it at all.

We reached the lift, but to our surprise the lift

was filled with the same poisonous gases which made us unconscious one by one. Somehow, we managed not to inhale those gases, but see how karma plays with you. We were stuck in the lift due to power failure; this happened when we couldn't bare the smell even for five minutes we had to bare it for another 10 minutes until the lift got functional.

Finally, we reached the room, but to our surprise there was another play of karma waiting. When we entered the room we jumped onto the bed, but still we could smell, the same thing which we experienced in the lift and looked at each other. We slowly followed the smell and to our surprise there he was our third-room mate in the washroom sitting relaxed and spreading the smell throughout the room.

We rushed, opened all the curtains and sprayed room freshener. Now we could finally breathe. When, he came out of the washroom we attacked him and he was our punching bag for that afternoon.

We all assembled in the hall for dining and we warned the third-room mate, Vishal, to be careful while having his dinner. Everyone's faces were looking dull and were like half-dead. There were a wide variety of dishes spread over the table. Every one of us silently sat and had our supper.

We took a stroll in the garden after a sumptuous dinner. There was silence for about 5 minutes, none of us spoke. We kept on walking and felt the nature. It was cool, I was wearing my blazer, she was feeling cold, so I just brought down my jacket and wrapped it around us. I didn't know why did I do so, but by doing this I had developed more feelings for her. There was a dim light in the garden and a bench to sit upon which gave us a view of the whole hotel. There were couples all over the hotel spending some quality with each other. It was the best time for romance.

We both sat there hand in hand for some time, but couldn't convey to each other. I dropped her at her room and went to bed.

The next day was an important one as we were scheduled to leave Thiruvananthapuram and go to Munnar, a hill station.

We were told to get ready by 7:00 am, but what happened next was very funny.

We slept at around 10:30 pm the day before, since we didn't want to miss the last day stay in Thiruvananthapuram. So, we decided to spend some time in the balcony deciding whether it was love or attraction. After a long thought we couldn't conclude anything.

Then we all went to bed at around 10:30 pm and forgot that next day we had to get up early. At around 6:00 am in the morning, the class-in charge had come to wake us up. She rang the doorbell, none of us responded. Then came the second ring and I was disturbed by that sound, so I told Akash to look who's at the door. He was already dreaming and responded with an *'Hmm'*. Now, there was the third door bell, unable to bear the third bell I kicked Vishal out of the bed and told him to check up. That fellow in return kicked me up and pushed me at the other end of the bed and jumped on the bed.

Now our door was being continuously banged and the door-bell rang. Unable to bear anymore three of us looked at each other and decided to go and thrash the asshole that was disturbing us. Akash went and opened the door, to our surprise the whole troop of nearly 70 students and 10 faculty members led by none other than Mr. Chatterjee were standing at the doorstep. We were stunned by seeing them.

There was the first question fired at us "*what's the time*". I laughed at first thinking why all had to come just to ask the time.

I replied in a casual way "*it's 8:30 am only sir*", Mr. Chatterjee gave me a stern look. Without any further questions everyone entered the room and checked the whole room. When they couldn't find anything, the second question was fired "*do you know what's today*", again I gave a broad smile and answered "*Sir you're kidding it's Monday*", and burst out laughing. By the time I stopped laughing a voice came from behind "*Sir, I think we should leave them here itself and go*".

There I got my senses back, recollecting I understood why all of them had gathered. We three apologized for the delay and rushed to get ready.

Finally, at around 10:30 am we left Thiruvananthapuram and all because of us. It was a five hour journey to Munnar. As we neared Munnar, the temperature dipped by 15 degree Celsius. Sivangi was tired and she rested her head on my shoulder. She looked cute while asleep just like a 5-year old innocent kid.

There were sharp turns on the road to Munnar. As, we were nearing Munnar the temperature kept on dipping. It was bitter cold. Sivangi was feeling cold, she was shivering, and so I closed the window and put my jacket over her. She came to normal.

It was around 7:00 in the evening when we reached Munnar. The temperature was around 2 degree Celsius. We got down and hurried to the room. The luggage was brought in and everyone was instructed to assemble at around 8:00 pm for dinner. We switched on the heaters in our room. Now everything was back to normal.

We had worn warm clothes with jackets on. The room was a large one with comfortable beds and the view outside the window was stunning. We were able to see those ghat roads with dim street light on the road. There was a beautiful full moon on the top of our hotel which gave an elegant look to the hotel.

We all gathered around 8:00pm and were served dinner. Everything served was hot and lip-smacking. The only problem there was that rice couldn't be eaten as it had some different kind of smell because the people in Kerala use coconut oil. Overall the food was good and tummy fillable.

After dinner there was a surprise for us, the camp-fire. There was a camp-fire set up in the forest area with live music. At first, everyone was nervous but once our principal along with Mr. Chatterjee started dancing; we too tapped our feet to the music. We danced in groups that meant one couple made one group. Everyone was brilliant with their partners. Sivangi and I forgot that people were around and started dancing like pros, seriously looking into each other's eyes. Everyone moved aside and looked at us; I lifted her up which was our last step. To our surprise everyone cheered and clapped and the atmosphere was filled with sounds of '*once more*'. We did it once again and this time nailed it.

After the dance we sat with our partners and were given space. I told Sivangi "*You are, too slim and I guess you are maintaining your figure*", she laughed aloud and said I hate the word figure. She said "*I love to be myself*", this touched somewhere deep inside my heart. I thought I had finally found someone who loved what she is.

The night was spent talking about ourselves, further goals and the endless jokes. We had fallen asleep into each other arms. The sun rose, the birds chirped, the smell of the wet mud woke us up. We then went to our respective rooms and got ready for the day.

The day was well spent; we were taken to the botanical garden. It was a beautiful morning, surrounded by flowers all over which gave more elegant look to the nature. We were shown various kinds of flowers and large, old trees. The garden was well maintained.

Later, during afternoon every one of us was provided with some sumptuous dishes spread over the table. The food for the day was far better than yesterday. After lunch we were given a small break. Read on to know what happened after the break....

Chapter 4: Life Gives A Twist

* * *

I know all the readers are eager to know what happened after the break. I too was left shocked with the thing that happened after the break. I had come to the conclusion of finally proposing Sivangi, but karma had some other plans in for me.

The first question asked to myself was *"Do, I seriously love her?"* The answer came was "*A big yes*".

The next question was "*Can I keep her happy?*" The answer was "*Yes, if I try*",

The next question was "*Will I be with her life long?*" I didn't have any answer for that.

The last question that came was "*Will she accept me?*" I was 50-50 about the answer.

After the break everything was going right when suddenly that evening we were about to leave for dinner and then something strange happened which gave me a second thought about life.

Every one of us strolled in the garden near the hotel. The scenery was beautiful, the sun setting and on the other end was the moon rising. We were told to get back to our room, get fresh and then to gather in the dining hall for dinner.

I remember the time, it was around 7:00pm and we all were about to leave, Sivangi was with me. I was talking to her when suddenly someone pulled her away it was Rohan, a classmate of mine. He got down on his knees and proposed Sivangi. I was left stunned by this.

She looked at me, he told her something in Telugu and to this everyone clapped and cheered. I guess it was some stupid proposing line. A tear rolled down my eyes, I couldn't bare him anymore, I was about to thrash him but Akash caught my hand and stopped me. I left the place with tears in my eyes. I could see my life shattered by his proposal.

I didn't wait for her answer to Rohan's proposal. I locked the room and cried my heart out. Someone knocked at my room. I didn't have the courage to open the door.

There were continuous knocks at the door. I helped myself and opened it. It was Rohan standing outside, he said in my ears "*Bro, she said yes*" the moment he said such I was fully broken.

Later, at dinner time Sivangi tried to approach me, I avoided her. I could see a tear roll down her eye when I avoided her and stopped talking to her. Akash came to me and said "*Bro, she didn't eat*" I replied very hastily "*What do you want me to do?*" how could she say yes to Rohan when she knew I like her. I too didn't have my dinner and zoomed to room.

Not my room, but her room. I wanted to know why she said yes to Rohan. I went to her room and knocked it three to four times. There was no response; I was worried what this mad girl might have done. Every minute that passed made me more nervous. Finally, she opened the door.

I walked in and went to the balcony, she followed. None of us spoke; we were looking at the view from balcony. There was a thick fog that covered the road; the moonlight was so bright that everything was visible without the help of any artificial lights. There was a slight rustling sound of leaves. Above us were the stars shining bright and calmness all over the forest.

We looked at each other. We did not speak our eyes spoke. By, now she too understood the reason of my arrival. I got her answer. We came close and she whispered in my ears "*I Love You, Only You*". Now we were at a distance where we could sense each other's breathe. Both of us were breathing at a faster pace, hearts too were racing at a faster pace. We looked into each other's eyes and closed it for a second. The lips met and now we were one soul two bodies. We deeply embraced each other. Only the nature spoke that night. The dim music being played outside and the cool breeze made the evening more romantic and full of life.

We were lost in some other world free from everything. Only Sivangi and me, suddenly we came back to the normal world when someone knocked at the door. It was Nanditha, Sivangi's best friend. Sivangi told me to wait; she wanted to tell Nanditha about our relationship. I stopped her from doing so. She was taken aback and asked me "*Why don't you want everyone to know we are in a relation*", I placed a finger on her lips and said "*I do want to tell the whole world that I love you, but at the correct time*".

By saying this I bid her goodbye and jumped off the window. We then met at the dinner table and had food as we were hungry after; a long and sweet kiss. It was like we were inseparable. After dinner we embraced each other and went to our respective rooms.

Akash and Faisal were waiting for me to arrive. There was good news awaiting Akash had proposed Sush and she too agreed. I didn't tell them my story. I wanted to give everyone a surprise.

Chapter 5: Love Blossoms

❄ ❄ ❄

That night was the last night in Munnar. I always would miss the fun in Munnar, but would take some lovely memories along with me.

Now, the last place to be visited in our 10 day schedule was Kanyakumari. I had planned each and everything and now it was my turn to shock Rohan.

The bus journey from Munnar to Kanyakumari was about 5-6 hours long. We got up early in the morning and packed our luggage, got into the bus after the breakfast. It was time to leave Munnar, the best place ever visited in my life with loads of sweet and a bitter memory.

Now we were heading to one of the best place in India, also called the tip of India, the Kanyakumari. On the way to Kanyakumari all of us were treated with coconut water, the famous drink in Kerala. The coconut water was sweet and yes the quantity of water too was much compared to the quantity we get in Hyderabad.

After about an hour's sleep, we were awoken by the sound of waves. Yes, finally we had reached Kanyakumari. We were able to see the waves touching the shore and many couples enjoying their best time. It was more fun when we got a three star hotel directly facing the Indian Ocean. All of us were on cloud nine.

The only problem was some of us got ocean facing rooms while the others did not get. So, a plan was made to allow everyone to enjoy the ocean view. Our schedule of Kanyakumari was for 4 days so each day one of them would shift along with their roommates to the ocean facing room and the next day the other and so on. Now, the problem was solved.

We rushed into the rooms and unpacked our luggage. We were told to get ready and meet at the dinner hall. All the boys had worn t-shirts with short tracks. We reached the dining hall on time, but as always, the girls were late.

Akash came up to me and said "*Bro, do you think me and Sush look good as a couple?*"

I told him "*Yes, but why did you get such a doubt*".

He blushed and nodded his head. Before we could further speak the ladies landed their footsteps on the ground. They were dressed in their best clothes. Sivangi was looking more gorgeous and romantic that evening.

I went up to her and asked "*Hey, gorgeous for whom did you dress this beautifully*".

The reply was "*Obviously not for you*", after hearing her reply both of us burst into laughter.

She was the best thing that happened in my life.

There were almost 50 dishes set up for dinner. These dishes were spread all over the table. We were now ready to attack. Every dish was lip-smacking ranging from starters to desserts. After having such a sumptuous dinner we were not able to move. We had become double of our weights.

Mr.Chatterjee was looking like the son of a sumo. His button had refused to close and the tummy was bulging out completely. One other item of food, had he ate his shirt would be torn. On, the other end the girls followed a strict diet to avoid looking overweight. The helped us with getting into the lift.

We all went to our rooms and dozed off. The next morning it was my turn to shift to the sea-facing room. What a coincidence it was, the same day Sivangi too shifted to the adjacent room. That day, our schedule was to visit the Vivekananda Statue located in the middle of the Indian Ocean. We were instructed to wear comfortable clothes, so that humidity would not make us feel sticky.

The boys had worn shorts with t-shirts and sunglasses. The girls had worn short denims with tops. Sivangi wore an elegant top. According, to me Sivangi was a versatile dresser. Every dress would fit perfectly onto her. Now, we boarded the bus which would take us to the sea shore.

Finally, we reached the sea shore and all of us were instructed about safety techniques. The ship was not too large to be called a cruise, but a medium one. We started clicking selfie with the light blue fresh water beneath us. The water was transparent up to a certain depth.

There was a large Swami Vivekananda's Statue visible in the middle of the ocean. We left for that place. Kanyakumari is the place where two seas join the Indian Ocean. All, of us were told to get down safely with the help of the ropes.

It was a large statue about 133 feet tall. Every one of us saluted the statue and felt proud to be born in a nation of great legends. We spent some time around the Memorial clicking pictures as these were the only source for our memories. After an hour we were told to be back at the same place where the ship had left us. Akash and I had not worn our watches that day.

All of our classmates had arrived at the departure place. The ship had arrived. Everyone got inside and when the ship was ready to depart Sivangi and Sush had not seen us in the ship. They went over to the captain of that ship and requested the ship to wait. They then started searching us in the ship. We both were busy looking at the waves, when suddenly someone placed a hand on us. It was Mr. Chatterjee; he had come to take us to the ship. We were apologetic for our mistake.

We reached the shore. Now, it was a tough task as the shore was almost 50 meters away and we had to reach the other side with the help of the rope. I was the last one to leave the ship; I landed my foot onto the rope, the captain not noticing I was on the rope, detached the rope from his end as he was already late for the next round. I fell into the water. At, the other end everyone was left shocked for about a minute. They were not able to believe what they had seen.

They reached for the authorities for help. Sivangi was crying sitting at the shore. All of them had tears in their eyes. When the authorities could not find anybody they returned back. They were sure that I was dead. I came from behind and placed a hand on Sivangi's shoulder and asked "*Why are you all crying, are all safe*", here other shock came their way.

I was alive and fit. I slipped into the waters and since it was no so deep I swam across and reached the shore from the other end. She slapped me and everyone started hitting me for frightening them. I reached the room and was advised to take rest.

We all were eagerly waiting for the evening, especially me. It was my turn to shock everyone. During the lunch time Sivangi had bought food to my room and fed me with her hands. I moved close to her and whispered in her ears "*I promise you that the evening would be the beautiful evening in your life*".

She replied "*I'm eagerly waiting for your surprise*". There was just two hours left for the surprise. In, the evening we were about to hit the beach and lots of surprises coming. Every one headed to the beach at around 5:00 pm. We were given safety instructions. Now, it was my turn to shock Rohan. All of us removed our footwear and headed to the beach. I told everyone to gather at the beach as I had some important news for them. Everyone gathered and was waiting for me to arrive.

I came and took Sivangi along with me. Everyone was awestruck when I got down on my knees and officially proposed Sivangi. I just said those three magical words "*I love you, do you?*"

She replied "I too love you". Everyone present there hooted and clapped. It was celebration time. Rohan was nowhere to be seen. Seeing us Akash too proposed Sush. I took Sivangi to the other side of the beach, the place over there is meant only for the couples.

I whispered in her ears "*Close your eyes, I have something for you*". She immediately shut her eyes.

When she opened her eyes, she felt something was attached to her neck. It was a locket with some of our memories in it. I told her "*The day I die you open this*". She placed her finger on my lips and said "*You just take me with you when you die*".

We looked at each other and smiled. The view

of the setting sun was exquisite. Only the sound of the water hitting the rocks could be heard. The dim light from the setting sun, the sound of the waves and the calmness of the beach made the evening more romantic. We moved close to each other, looked at each other and with hand in hand started dancing. The birds flew over the ocean and the wind was blowing at the slightest speed. We kissed each other. It was like the whole nature was happy with our relationship; we bowed to thank them for such a memorable evening. The dim light coming from the sun started fading and the streetlights were switched on.

We were in some other world where there was no basis of caste, religion, color and complexion. The only thing that mattered in that world was only love. They say and love has no caste, creed and religion. We were a free bird.

It was time for us to come back to this world and join our troop. We played the whole evening, splashed water onto each other, swam and enjoyed our hearts out. It was a memorable evening. I had finally found my love, got a great gang of friends, life was smooth.

The following day we went shopping. I purchased a few toys for my sister's and yes a teddy for my beautiful partner. She loved it and thanked me by pecking on my cheeks. She too had a gift for me. It was a beautiful silver locket. She too said the same thing in my ears "*Open it only after I die*".

It was the last day of our stay in Kanyakumari. The next day we boarded the train and were heading to Hyderabad. We reached Hyderabad after a long and tedious journey of about 28 hours in the train. Dad and uncle had come to pick me at the station, her parents too had come. So, it was now time for us to bid goodbye to each other.

Chapter 6: The Last Goodbye

* * *

I was excited to meet her next day at school. Finally, I was relieved to get a partner who understands me well and never complains.

I went home distributed gifts among my brothers & sisters, told them about the beauty of Kerala and many other things. My naughty brother, Vinit missed my company for these days and complained about the same. It was dinner time when I finally completed telling them about the journey. We all were having dinner when my phone buzzed, it was Sivangi calling me. As I was with my family I couldn't lift her call.

There was a continuous buzz on my phone. I saw there were 15 missed calls of her when I tried to call her back, she lifted the call and all I could hear was "*I love you*" and then the call was cut. When I tried to call back there was a voice message which said "*The number you are calling is not reachable*".

I couldn't sleep the whole night and tried calling her back, but there was no response from the other end. I was worried every single minute that passed by brought many weird thoughts in my mind. The first thing that I planned to do the next morning was going to her place.

I got up and hurried myself because I couldn't wait anymore, rushed myself to the bicycle stand. From there I went to her apartment and to my surprise there was a lock on the door. Then when I inquired from their neighbors I got to know that they had vacated the flat and were rushing somewhere.

I had tears in my eyes; I looked for her but failed to find her. When I couldn't find her I just got down on my knees and looked up at the sky and questioned God "*Why did you do this to me?*" With tears in my eyes I reached the school.

There her best friend was waiting for me. She ran up to me and handed me some photographs, these photographs were of mine and Sivangi. She told me that Rohan had clicked them and started blackmailing Sivangi. When she refused to accept him, he sent those photos to Sivangi's dad. After seeing those photos, Sivangi's dad planned to call up the police, but Sivangi somehow managed to cool her dad down by promising him that she will not be meeting me anymore. They now have shifted to some other state without telling anyone.

Hearing all these things I couldn't stop the tears rolling down my cheeks. She tried to console me, but I had mixed emotions; one side I had anger on Rohan and the other end I was all alone she was gone, long gone.

Every time I recalled her; only three words went through my mind, the last three words said by her "*I love you*". Whenever I recalled those words, tears rolled down by eyes. I lived just hoping one day I would come across her.

By this, I understood one thing when something really good happens in your life so suddenly, then there is really bad going to arrive.

My situation was like that of a person who is left

out all alone in a crowd. I was trying to be optimistic about meeting her someday, somewhere, sometime.

I helped myself and thought of moving ahead in my life. My brother, Vinit used to be always with me in thick and thin. The bad phase of my life was gone and yes, it took me time to recover.

Now, it was time for the Final Examinations, the boards. I had been preparing hard to secure a good percentage. After the boards everyone partied with their girlfriends. Since I had none I partied with my family members. Later, I met all my school friends for the last time. We all hugged and promised to regularly be in touch with each other. All of us thanked our teachers for bearing with us for almost 10 years. There were emotions, happiness and memories. The emotions were of us leaving each other's company. The happiness was that all of us were starting the new phase of life.

With many promises made and loads of memories we bid farewell to the most beautiful phase of life.

Chapter 7: The New Phase Of Life

* * *

The sun rose and with this beautiful sunrise started my new phase of life. The career promising phase called as the intermediate phase. We were told that these 2 years of intermediate would decide our future and all. I was eager to enter this new phase of my life and see what it has for me in it.

I had secured admission in one of the best and career promising college The Chaitanya College with the course MPC. It had a twin brother as its competitor in the market The Narayana College. Every year they outsmarted the public by portraying themselves as the No.1 Institute. They promise classes from morning 9:00 till late in the evening up to 6:30pm. My parents too dreamt of me being an engineer whose parent's don't, so they thought these institutes would provide me the best education.

It was my first day of college. Since everything was new for me, dad had come to drop me. He told me to concentrate on studies for these two years were the life changing moment of my life. Like any other kid, I too nodded my head and left for my class.

Since it was the first day the corridors were crowded as everyone were looking out for their respective classes. After struggling for about 15 minutes I too found my class. The class was already crowded, some of them knew each other before itself, some students like me were new and others sat alone, they were a kind of reserved.

I went and took a seat in the second bench. The teacher arrived. We were told to introduce ourselves. After the introduction class we got to know each other.

It was the recess hour when a girl was walking towards our class and all of the boys were like bro she's mine. All of us were awestruck by her beauty. She came to the class and introduced herself as our mathematics teacher. We still couldn't believe that she is our mathematics teacher. Her name was different from others. She introduced herself as Ms. Lovely. Some back benchers began hooting and shouting.

The class went on and then something unusual happened. A boy from our class jumped out of the window in the middle of the class. I thought "*How would someone have guts to do that on the very first day of college*". Ms. Lovely too was left stunned.

During our lunch hour, I went up to him and asked his name, he answered me with a smile "*Hi I am Nikhil*".

I was eager to know why he jumped out of the window and raised that question to him. He calmly replied "*I was bored of that class*" seeing my doubtful face, he continued further "*I just don't want to waste my life studying, yes of course I do have some ambitions and goals, but those are useless without any memories. I just have a dream which I think you're the first one I'm sharing with*".

This made me more anxious, I asked him "Bro, what's your dream?"

He replied "*When I die, my certificates, my awards and rewards don't matter, the only thing that matters is the memories which I leave behind*". His way of thinking inspired me. He was calm, friendly and full of live.

I went home happily as I had found a new friend who was a bit crazy and had similar thoughts like mine. The next day I was excited to go to college. He was sitting there all alone. I went to him and said "*Can I have a seat beside you?*"

He was like "*Bro, you are my good friend, you can sit beside me*". This day we were introduced to some new lecturers. Among all the lecturers the best one was our English lecturer Mr. Bijli. At first we too thought it to be a female lecturer, but god knows how a male happened to be with such a name. His nature was friendly, but the best part was his English accent. He always made faces while speaking in English. We used to laugh by saying "Bijli, *gir gayi*".

The first few days were spent on knowing each other. A few days later the real torture started, we were told that every weekend we would have tests conducted based on the portion of the week. We all were annoyed by the announcement. There was an iron gate being put up in front of each class. It was like a prison where we were the prisoner's and the lecturer's the jailers. We were detached from the outside world.

Every one of us was provided with a set of study materials. One fine day during the lunch hour a girl came downstairs. She had worn a parrot colored dress. Her smile reminded me of Sivangi. Her looks were alluring.

Seeing her, the words that came out of my mouth

were "*What a beauty*!" I could hear someone utter the same thing from behind. When I turned back it was Haloon, a smelly, fatty, chubby, hairy friend of mine. Hairy meant he had full grown hairs all over the body and whenever he would sweat there would be some different kind of odor coming from his body to which everyone would try to escape. The smell reminded me of Mr. Chatterjee.

Now, we both were staring at each other. This was the point where the challenge came up. The challenge was that whoever woos the girl first, he wins. Now we were busy preparing our respective strategies.

She would daily come downstairs to the canteen during the recess hour. I used to stare her from the window and Haloon from the corridor. She would stare both of us. The big question was who does she like?

Nikhil was confident she was staring at me and some other boys were confident it was Haloon. I was in no hurry, but Haloon was.

I spoke to her after college hours. I asked her name, she was a kind of shy girl. At first she didn't reply, but later she introduced herself as Priya. We exchanged our numbers and began chatting.

A week later Haloon came up to me and said "*Bro, I have her number*". I kept quiet and gave him a smile. Now, both of us were going strong.

We had decided that we would propose her on the eve of Teacher's day. It was just a week away. All of us began decorating the classes. There was basically a competition that whichever classroom would be elegantly decorated would win a prize.

Every one of us began working hard on it. On the other hand it was our D-Day.

Finally, the Teacher's day arrived and we had almost completed our decoration. We were informed to hurry up because by 9:30 the principal and other faculty members would inspect each and every class and thereupon decide the winner.

We gave our best and were hoping to be the winner. Yes, it actually happened our wish came true. Our class Neon-IC won the first price. Every one of us was in celebratory mood. I could see Haloon rush behind Priya.

Both of them went upstairs. I took Nikhil along with me and went behind them. I couldn't believe what my eyes had seen. Haloon got down on his knees with a white coat on and with a bunch of red roses proposed Priya.

He said "*You're the most beautiful girl I had ever met. I promise to fulfill all your wishes. Do you love me?*"

I was like is this the way you propose a girl? She quietly replied "*Thank you for the red roses, but you're not of my type*". Hearing her answer I giggled. He came downstairs with an upset face. Now, it was my turn to propose her. But before I could do, there was something which shocked me even more.

I was ready to go upstairs and propose her but; before I did so Nikhil took me to the washroom and told me a shocking thing. When we were busy wooing her, she proposed to Nikhil. However Nikhil's sister rejected Priya and cautioned Nikhil about her character.

He told me "*Bro, she is a characterless girl; if am not wrong she already lost her virginity*". The last line gave me a setback. He advised me to drop out of the challenge. I gave up the challenge but still couldn't believe what I heard. In order to confirm this I was heading upstairs, I could hear someone breathing heavily.

To my surprise it was Priya who was kissing a senior guy. I said to myself "*Thank you God for saving me from such a Bitch*".

I came down and we started celebrating our win. We tapped our feet to the music. We took a break and helped ourselves with some snacks and soft drinks. The cap of the bottle was stuck and it became difficult to open.

I tried my best and pulled off the car. The cap opened, only after dirtying Haloon's white coat. His white coat had now turned black.

He said "*Bro, what should I tell at home?*" I took the coat from him, promised to dry wash and return it to him.

Chapter 8: The Coat Case

* * *

The days passed by and I completely forgot about the incident. One day he came up to me and asked "*Hey dude, how's the coat now?*"

I replied hastily like I had no idea about the coat "*Which coat are you talking about?*"

He replied, "*The one which you had taken by promising me to get it dry washed*". I replied "*Oh! That one, yes it's almost done*".

I could see him smile, he hugged me and thanked me for the work. He told me he needed it urgently as he was about to attend a marriage the day after.

Now, it was tough times ahead for me. I ran home and searched for his coat, but couldn't find it anywhere. Taking a deep breath, I sat on the chair and recollected the incidents. Suddenly I was like "*Oh shit! How could I forget it in the college?*" Yes, I had kept his coat in the class itself; it was over there from over a month.

I just ran as fast as my legs could and reached the college only to see the gates closed. Looking at the sky, I asked "*Why God, why do you always do this to me*". Again a bad game played by karma.

The only thing I could do was to wait for the sunrise. I went home dejected and slept. Thank god karma didn't have the powers to stop the sun from rising and setting.

The very next day my first goal of the day was Mission Coat. I somehow managed to take the coat and put it in a cover.

Meanwhile Haloon came to me and said "*Bro, I know everything. There's nothing left to hide*". At first I was left stunned, I asked him "*You know everything?*"

He replied "*Yes, I do*". I was pretty sure that it was Game-Over for me.

I kept calm and replied "*I was about to tell you but didn't know how you would react*".

Haloon replied "*I didn't expect this from you. I thought you would speak the truth*".

In a slow, soothing tone I said "*I'm sorry*". He hugged me and said "*Don't worry, Nikhil told me everything*". I looked at Nikhil; he was standing in the corridor and smiling at me. He had booked me very badly.

He continued further, "*You didn't propose Priya and gave up the challenge that day itself. Nikhil told me each and everything that happened that day and yes about her character too. You chill now*".

I replied "*Oh, you were talking about that incident. Holy Shit*", saying this I laughed. He got a doubt and asked "*Yes, were you expecting something else*". To which I said "*No, I was expecting this*".

Finally, I was relieved, but even before I could take a deep breath, he reminded me that next day he needed the Coat. I smiled at him and said "*It will be ready by tomorrow*".

That evening I hurried home like hell. I put some detergent into a bucket of water and let the Coat soak in it for some period of time. After about an hour, still the patch was visible. It was a month-old patch and no such detergent was launched in the market yet which would remove a month-old stains.

I tried to brush off the stain, but that went in vain. There was no other option left except dry-cleaning. I ran to the dry-cleaning shop and said "*Bhaiyya yeh coat dry-clean karkey thoda urgently hona*". He looked at me and said "*Beta, yeh 2 days mey hoga issey jaldi to mein kya bhagwan bhi nahi kar sakta*".

With no other way left, I ran to the terrace and put it on the wire to allow it to dry. Even there Karma didn't support me, the sun had set. Now there was only one option left, switch on the fan in my room and let the coat dry over there. I went to the room, switched on the fan to the top speed and let the Coat dry, by placing it on the chair.

Every hour I went to the room to check whether it dried or not and as usual returned disappointed. Only prayers could help me in that situation, just hoping everything would be fine the next morning.

The sun rose, but still the coat remained wet. I ironed it hoping the steam would let the water ooze out of the Coat. The outcome was terrible; there was some strange smell coming from the Coat, the smell was similar to the drainage one. I put the still some wet Coat into a cover and took it to the college.

I could see Haloon waiting for me at the gate; with a wide smile he hugged me. I handed him the cover and told him not to open it till he reaches his home. He asked "*Why don't you want me to open it*".

I replied calmly "*Bro, it's ironed, if you take the Coat out then the ironed Coat might get damaged*". He nodded and promised me to open the coat once he reached him. I told this incident to Nikhil and he too laughed his heart out.

The classes went as usual, but I didn't pay attention to any of them as my mind was full of fear, as to how he would react once he sees the coat. I told to myself "*Start preparing the forgiveness lines*".

In the evening I reached home and was waiting for his call, till then I had memorized the forgiveness line. As expected, he called me.

I took the call and started "*Hey bro how's the Coat*". There was no response from the other end, it was all silent. Then came a voice "*Hello, do you think this Coat's mine*".

I replied "*Yes, it's yours*". He said "*Bro, it's all wet and stinking. Did you seriously dry-clean it*"?

Taking a deep breath I confidently replied "*Yes, I even paid him RS.272/- for the work*".

He replied "*Just a minute and there was complete silence for over a minute*". For that one whole minute I held my breath.

Then a voice came from other end, it was a women's voice "*Hello beta mai Haloon ki mom baath kar rahi hun*".

I said "*Hello aunty, aap kaisey hai?*"

From the other end I could hear aunty scream at Haloon. She told him to shut up and sit. I thought it was my turn. Aunty started "*Beta, can you show me the bill, Haloon was telling you gave it to dry-cleaning.*"

I replied "*Aunty I don't have the bill right now, it's all right I already paid the bill*".

The next question was fired "*Where do you stay? Give me your address, I will come to your place along with Haloon*".

I politely replied "*Aunty why do you take the*

pain of coming to my place, it's far long. Also, I am going out for a function and yes I am sorry about the Coat".

She was stubborn about coming to my place, she said "*Just give me your address; I want to come to your place and meet the dry-cleaner who washed the Coat in this way*".

I again told the same thing "*I am going out and won't be at home. If you want, you can still come, I'll take you to the dry-cleaner*". She could sense the confidence in my words and replied "*I know it's not your fault beta, thank you for doing so much*".

There ended the conversation and this time my confidence helped me. I looked at the sky and thanked god for helping me out of it. That night I slept peacefully.

The next morning humming songs, I entered the classroom only to find Haloon sitting and staring at me with red blood eyes. The first thing I did was took off my earphones and sat beside him. None of us spoke. After a while he said "*Bro, did you seriously dry-wash it?*" I confidently said "*Yes, why did something happen*".

He angrily replied "*What not happened. I was thrown out of the house and spent the whole night on the terrace without food. There were bloody mosquitoes which didn't even allow me to sleep peacefully*".

Then next thing I asked was "*Did you take bath?*" He looked at me and said "*Yes, I did that too on the terrace itself at 4:00 am in the morning*". I replied "*I am sorry bro*". He said the story didn't end here. I said go no as if it was a movie.

He continued "*In the morning, Mom told me to come down and ordered me to clean the whole house. When I did with a lot mistakes she hit me with the broom and then finally I was given food*". I giggled and said "*I can understand the pain bro*". I know I was being sarcastic. He forgave me when I showed him my hand made receipt.

Everything went smooth after the incident. The whole class was like a family to me. During the classes Nikhil and I had a unique way of talking to each other. We used to talk by writing behind our notebooks which was passed to each other. It was fun and we were never caught.

As our bond of friendship grew stronger day by day the same way our Intermediate exams were nearing day by day. We were now busy preparing for our exams.

As planned the exams went very well. It was vacation time and I along with my family left for Shirdi. There I just asked for one thing a good result.

It was the month of June and everyone was tensed since it was result day. I didn't even have my breakfast. Everyone in my family was surfing different sites. It was around 11:30 am when the result was declared. I put down my hall-ticket number and was waiting for the result. The screen displayed 85% with 'A' grade. It was celebration time as my sister who was the same age as of mine secured 97%. We congratulated each other and then started the celebrations. Everyone from my class had got a good percentage and was promoted to the second year. I called up Nikhil and congratulated him. We both had secured the same percentage. The college was to reopen on 15th of June.

On the 15th of June we would officially be called as senior students of our college. There was a large banner put outside the college with the photos of the toppers on it. Again, the same advertisements were shown where both the Chaitanya and Narayana called themselves as the No.1 Institutes.

Chapter 9: The Fun Filled Year

* * *

The most awaited and career deciding year had arrived i.e. the second and final year of our intermediate life. We were officially the seniors, it was fun being seniors. On the other hand there was a whole bag of responsibilities on us. At the end of the second year all of us were to appear for various competitive exams which would play a major role in the future.

Amidst all these responsibilities we didn't want to spoil the final year of our intermediate life.

It was the first day of our second year. As usual, there was a new bunch of faculty members who introduced themselves. They gave a lecture on various career opportunities and the amount of hard work we had to do. All of us nodded their heads as if we really understood what he had said.

We were now separated from the juniors. Our classes were shifted to the other block. Only MPC and BPC students were accommodated in the block.

The classes began and on the other hand the fun too. Every week there were Eamcet and JEE Mains exams being conducted. We were taken to the principal's cabin after every week's result. The only thing the principal would say was "*improve, improve*".

The starting few months were spent getting used to these tortures. Slowly we started bunking the classes. Since, we were seniors there was no fear of message being sent to our parents. Once we happened to bunk the class and went to Fox Sagar, it was a triple ride. We took the service road, hoping we wouldn't get caught. We were lucky enough to have taken the service road.

Fox Sagar is a small lake surrounded by thick vegetation. It is a romantic spot for the couples. Each and every couple visits the place to spend some quality time with their partners. We had no girlfriends, so we decided to spend some quality time among ourselves.

It was the best place to visit during the monsoon season. After spending some time at the place, we were refreshed. Now, it was time to return back. We were too hungry so we planned to have something on the way and then go to college.

We left Fox Sagar and took the service road. To our surprise there were *mamas* standing waiting for us. Since we were triple riding, we were told to stop by the traffic police constable.

He asked us "*License bathao*". As we were under 18 at that age, we didn't have a license and RC, added to that we were ridding tricky. He was busy making a challan against our vehicle when we approached him.

Nikhil went and spoke to him. He directed us to the inspector who was sitting in the car. We went to him and said "*Sir, we are students, please forgive us*".

He replied "*Kitna hai utna de do*". We searched our pockets and altogether managed to collect RS.70/-. We went to him and said "*Sir, we have 70/- please take it*". Seeing the money he laughed and replied "*kisko dera 70/-, usmmey kya hota*".

The very next moment there was a challan issued against the vehicle and the vehicle was taken to the nearest police station. We too went along with it. On the way there were several calls made to our friends who we thought would help us in that situation. None of them were available.

We went to the police station; sitting there Nikhil called up one of his friends who promised to arrange money. It was not a small sum. On the other end Sainath's dad was continuously ringing him. It was his dad's vehicle and as it was lunch time his dad needed the vehicle. His dad called him continuously. He was in a situation where he couldn't answer the call. He was tensed and every single minute passing by, was scaring the hell out of him. After about half an hour the screen read "*32 missed calls*".

His dad was a strict person. Finally a message read on the screen "*Beta, get the bike in the evening as I had my lunch*". Now, we were relieved. It was the first time I visited a police station. The environment over there was calm.

Then after about 3 hours of waiting, Nikhil's friend brought the amount. We thanked him and cleared the challan. His friend left and now we were damn hungry but penniless. Even after this incident, we didn't change ourselves. We went triple riding to the college. We rushed into the class to collect our bags and went home.

The following day Sainath came with a swollen eye. When we inquired about his injury, he replied "*Nothing much dad just had a boxing match with me*". By this we understood imagined yesterday's scenario at his place.

A few days later during the recess hour we were busy staring the dumb faced BIPC girls. My eyes caught something, it was a beautiful girl. Her smile made everyone got mad. Those cute dimples on her cheek and the million dollar smile were elegant. The first word that came off my mouth was "*I love her*". The same could be heard from behind me. Guess who it might be. Yes, it was none other than that asshole Haloon.

I gave him a stern look. Looking at my look he said "*She's yours, I back out*". Nikhil saw me staring her and said "*Bhai, she had no boyfriend before and the ones who proposed her got rejected*". I was like "*That's interesting*". Now I had another goal in my bucket of goals. She was my goal.

Nikhil was ready to help me since it was a complicated case. Many of them told me, that she was a studious girl and wasn't interested in all these stuffs. I had made up my mind, if I propose anyone it would be only she, else's no one.

A few days passed by, I spent these days staring at her. She knew I was staring her and she didn't mind, me doing so. During the recess hour news broke out which shook the whole campus. The news was a new section was proposed which would have only a limited number of students. The students would be selected based on the result of the exam, which was to be conducted in the coming weekend.

The whole second year was preparing for the exam. Nikhil and I just gave a reading of the topics and left for the exam. The exam was a tough one.

The results were to be declared the following day. Only 15 students from our class got selected which included Nikhil and me. We were overjoyed not because we were selected, but on the fact that we would meet many different beauties in the class.

Among all the new girls from different sections, there she was, my dimpled smile girl. I didn't know her name yet and it was fun to call her '*dimpled smile girl*'. The classes went on from morning 6:00 till late in the evening 7:00. It was time for some change, so we planned something different.

Chapter 10: Mission Dimpled Smile

* * *

Since, we were bored of these classes we planned a mission. Days passed on and I was attracted more and more towards her and the silly thing was I didn't even know her name.

This time Karma was by my side. One day Nikhil came running at me as if he had seen some ghost. Coming to me he said "*Bhai, bhabhi ka naam patha chala*".

I asked him "*Jaldi bol salley*". He was like "*I won't tell the name unless you treat me somewhere*". I had to shell out a minimal amount of 500/- to know her name. Her name was Akanksha, the dimpled smile girl.

The first thing I did after reaching home was that I sent her a friend request on Facebook. The very next moment there was a message on the computer screen which read "*Friend request accepted*". I was overjoyed with the message.

Then the chat began. I asked her, "*Do you know me?*" and she took some time to reply and said "*You're the one who continuously stares at me*". I was like "*Yeah, you're so beautiful that I couldn't resist myself*". The chats went on like about our likes and dislikes and future goals.

Day by day the chats grew and a bond of friendship developed between us. On the other end that asshole Nikhil had already found his lady love. It was Nakshatra our classmate. They both had been seeing each other from the 1st year itself and now finally he dared to propose her. I was the only one left without a girlfriend.

Akanksha, Nakshatra, Nikhil and I became a great gang. We used to hang out on a regular basis. One thing I liked about Akanksha was that she was an adamant devotee of Sai Baba. Every Thursday she would visit the temple and offer prayers. As days passed our bond of friendship was turning into love. She knew I liked her, but I wasn't sure if she did.

The mid-term examinations were scheduled in the month of December. We were busy preparing for mid-terms and didn't know how the days passed by. The exams were over and we were given a Christmas vacation, which was a week long. Nikhil and I had planned about the New Year Eve. We invited Akanksha and Nakshatra to the party. At first they refused, but after a lot of pleading, they agreed to come.

Finally the day arrived, which I was eagerly waiting for, the 30th of December, the last day of the year. We were scheduled to leave for the party at around 8:00 PM. I picked up Akanksha and Nikhil and Nakshatra in the car. We tapped our feet's the soulful romantic music which was played that evening. At around 11:00 PM the phone rang. It was Nakshatra's dad; he was a short tempered person. Her dad ordered Nakshatra to reach home by 11:30, so we left the party in between. I was frustrated as nothing was going according to the plan.

We dropped the girls at their place and left for my home. I sat on the terrace looking at the stars and said "Why does this always happen to me?" The question was left unanswered. At around 12:00 a group of friends bumped at my place to celebrate the New Year. I didn't want to celebrate the year without her. My phone buzzed, it was Akanksha.

I picked up the call "*Happy New Year Dumbo*" was what she said. I replied "*Happy New Year*". The clock was exactly pointing at 12:00 and without wasting a single minute I just spoke out the three golden words "*I love you*". There was complete silence at the other end. I looked at my phone thinking '*Did she cut my call?*'

The silence was interrupted by a soft, lovely voice from the other end "*I love you too*". It was exact 12:00 when she said these three words. I couldn't believe my ears. I was going crazy over this and continuously kept on saying "*I love you*" and from the other end these words were repeated. It was a memorable thing for both of us. I guess there would be only a few couples who would have had such memories.

I was like on cloud nine. We spoke to each other till 3:00 in the morning. She told me each and everything about her and expected the same from me. At one point she got emotional, she said "*Vipul, I lost my mother at an early age and saw my dad go through many problems. It's very tough to live without a mother. If I would break down, then who would take care of my dad, so I was being strong these many years and you came into my life. Just promise me one thing that you will never leave me and go please, I love you*".

This thing brought tears to my eyes. It taught me one important lesson of life. If you have everything, you'll take it for granted, but once you start losing them, then you'll realize what important role they played in your life. I promised never to leave her.

The time went on and we didn't realize that it was already 6:00 in the morning. It was beautiful morning for both of us and with a lovely sunrise started our new love journey.

Later, we bid each other goodbye and cut the call. When I turned back there was that asshole Vishnu sleeping with his tongue out and saliva oozing out of his mouth. I pulled out a bucket of water from the tank and poured over him. He got up and said "*I'm sorry baby*", I was like "*Baby nahi baap bol baap*".

I dropped him to his place and came back home. The night had changed me completely. I went to have a shower when suddenly a phone beeped. There was a message which read, "*Baby, I have a surprise for you come home*". I dressed up and took Nikhil along with me. I didn't know the route and after about half an hour of roaming in the similar lanes we found her house. It was beautiful from outside. There was a large entrance with a small garden and a fleet of cars in the garage. She came out wearing a sari. She was looking damn hot. She called me near her and told me to close my eyes. I went towards her with my lips moving much more forward than my footsteps. Seeing me coming this way she giggled and told me to kiss it. I was pretty excited and kissed it. The kiss burned my lips, it wasn't her lips, instead she handed me a tiffin box and hurriedly left promising to give me something else next time.

With burning lips I too left her place. We then headed to Nikhil's place and opened the tiffin. The aroma of the food made us crazy. I took a spoon and had the first bite. It was lip smacking, to be frank she was a much better than my mom. We fought till the last morsel.

My phone rang and it was Akanksha at the other end. I picked her call and thanked her for such a sumptuous meal. She said "*Tell me really, did you like it*" to which I replied "*Yes babe it was yummy and I loved it, if you were here I would have had kissed your hands. Such a great cook you are*".

We spoke for about few minutes and then later I went home and slept. The following day was the last day of the special section. We were given useful tips on cracking the competitive exams.

That night she called me around 2:00, at first I was shocked to see her call and answered it. The first question was "*Is everything fine baby?*" She replied "*Yes, every thing's fine. I wasn't feeling sleepy so called you up. Did I disturb you by doing so?*"

With a sigh of relief I answered "*No your call didn't disturb*" by saying this I slept. When I woke up in the morning the call wasn't cut. Thinking she was still awake I said "*Good morning*" but to my surprise I could hear her snoring. I smiled and decided to record her snoring.

Finally, we were back to our class and were just 2 months away from our finals. It was lab time and we were busy in doing our experiments when Nikhil called me out. He said "*Bro, I need your help*" to which I replied "*Yes sure anytime*". He took Nakshatra and went to the adjacent lab. He told me to stand out and inform him if someone came.

After about 15 minutes both of them came out and were serious. I went to Nikhil and said "*Bhai aisa kya Kara jisey bhabhi serious hogayi*". He replied "*Bro we had some small issue on which we both fought*" Without any further delay, I fired another question "*then what did u do*" He gave a broad smile and said '*nothing*'.

I said to myself "*yeh kabhi nahi sudhrega*". The next day Haloon came up to me saying "*Bro, Akanksha is already in relation!*" I wanted to fool him so I put out a face as if I didn't know anything. I replied "*What! Oh no phir sey tera bad luck*". He replied by correcting me and said "*Not only have my bad lucked, even yours too*". I gave him a stern look and replied "*Ya, why don't you go and ask Akanksha her boyfriend's name*", saying this I left and stood at one corner of the gate talking to Nikhil.

Akanksha came down along with her friend. As soon as she stepped down that clumsy fatso ran towards her with his booty shaking and the pant slipping. Nikhil and I were looking at him. Half of his booty was visible from behind. Standing there he directly asked her "*What's the name of your boyfriend?*" She replied interestingly "*You already know him*" His face had become smaller in size. Adjusting his pant he replied "*where is your boyfriend?*" She calmly said "*he is right behind you*"

He came to me with a large wide opened mouth and asked "*Are you in relation with Akanksha*" With a broad smile I replied "*yes*" and then patting on his shoulder Nikhil and I left.

The lab internals were scheduled in the month of January itself, so wasting no further time we get busy preparing for these internals.

The best part in Inter is lab internals. We were a bit worried because it was the first time we were giving lab internals. We mugged up aim and procedure. We went formally dressed. I had worn a white shirt with a black formal pant. My number was called. I was told to pick up a chit, closing my eyes, I picked up a chit, this time I could call myself lucky.

The experiment was an easy one. I wrote the aim and procedure. The others were struggling. Then something interesting happened. The external was taken out for breakfast.

Later, after about an hour the external arrived. We were told to perform the practical. The experiment which I had got was Simple pendulum, having no idea what should be done, I simply started moving the pendulum and noted down the oscillations. I could see the external walking towards me briskly. I moved the pendulum faster, as his footsteps neared the pendulum became even faster.

Finally, at a point the pendulum landed at the feet of the external. I could see him crying in pain. The leg had swollen and he was immediately taken for medication. Everyone in the room was happy seeing the external going away. They thanked me from the depth of their hearts. That day I came to know about the hidden talent in me.

Chapter 11: The Valentine's Month

* * *

We were now done with the externals. It was February commonly known as the valentine's month. The whole week had something special in itself. Nikhil and I thought it would be fun celebrating the whole week with our partners. When we were planning about what should be done the whole week when we were interrupted by a call. The call was from my home and after attending the call I left in a hurry.

Later, I had to leave for Bangalore to attend a cousin's wedding. The event was about five days long. The whole family was scheduled to leave on 10th and the return date was 15th, I told the same to Akanksha. Her reply was a page long, so let me tell you it in short, she meant "do as you wish". I knew this would hurt her, but I didn't have any other option.

When I told the same to Nikhil, his reply was as expected "*Ja bey salley shaadi mey jakar ghanta maar aur wapas math aana*". Nikhil insisted to come along with me to the station. I went to the station; the train was scheduled to depart by 5:30pm. We had arrived almost an hour before the departure. I went to put my luggage and came out. We took a stroll around the station. He asked me just one question "*Sacchi bol kab takh wapas ara?"* I replied "*Bro, I will be back by 16th*" he was unhappy with my answer.

When I turned back to leave I could see a girl running towards me. Yes, it was Akanksha. She came to me and hugged tightly, she then whispered in my ears "*Are you seriously going? Is it necessary for you to go?*" I replied "*Yes*".

Without speaking any further she left. I could feel my shoulders were wet. Till I could turn around and call for her, she was long gone. This thing reminded me of some similar incident the one that happened with me a couple of years ago.

Then, suddenly the alarm rang. It was 6:00 in the morning. The dream was a horrifying one and the worst nightmare I had ever had. There was a message from Akanksha. I unlocked the screen and the message read "*Baby, I'm leaving for Bangalore to attend my cousin's wedding and would be back within a couple of days*". The first question I asked her was "*Are you going by train*" to which she replied "*No, I'll be going by flight*".

I was relieved by her answer, wishing her happy journey and after getting a couple of lovely kisses over the phone I left for college. Since, it was my first valentine I had no clue about it. I just wanted to give a sweet surprise to the love of my life.

I was half-way in my dream when the phone buzzed. I lifted the call and answered in dizzy tone "*Who is it?*" then a girl whispered at the other end "*Baby*" I replied sarcastically "*I'm still a virgin and have no babies*". I could hear the girl laugh aloud and the call was cut. I was like "*Who the hell was it*".

When I checked my phone it was Akanksha's call. I called her back and we wished each other "*A hap-*

py Valentine" and continued our 2 AM talks. She was scheduled to leave Bangalore at around 9:00 am and would reach Hyderabad by 11:00 am. We bid each other goodbye with lovely phonic kisses.

I then freshened up and left for college. The third hour was going on when the phone buzzed with a message which read "*Baby no one's at home, if you can then come at my place for lunch*". I waited for the period to get over and once the bell rang, I ran as if some mad bull was behind me.

I called up Nikhil and told him to come to the college at the earliest. He arrived hurriedly and upon seeing me outside the college, he asked "*kya hua? Suspend karey?*" I was like stop your shitting jokes, its valentine and we need to shop something for our partners.

He took me to Archie's; it is a famous gifting store. We went in and checked for the items which were affordable. We came across such gifts which were affordable, unique and hoped that our partners would like it. We packed the gifts in a unique warp and left.

Nikhil dropped me at Akanksha's place and headed to Nakshatra's home. She had recently shifted to an apartment as her house was getting renovated. Her dad had left for office early as he had to attend some meeting and would not return till late night.

I opened the gate and went upstairs. Her apartment was on the first floor. I went and knocked the door. The door was opened only after about 10 minutes of continuous knock. I could see nothing as the lights were turned off and the hall was dark. I was like a bit frightened and called out Akanksha for about 10 times, there was no response.

I somehow reached till the hall when suddenly

I could hear something burst above my head with the lights turning on. A beautiful girl in a rose red dress came to me and whispered "*Do you love me?*" I replied "*yes*" with that reply another surprise enfolded, the surprise was Nikhil and Nakshatra. I went to Nikhil and welcomed him with a blow. He said "*Kyun maara?*" I replied "*Bro this is my surprise*".

It was cake time. Akanksha and Nakshatra had together baked the cake. It contained four different flavors. We cut the cake and then it was dance time. We tapped our feet's to some lovely romantic music. At one point Nikhil and I got down on our knees and proposed our partners, the proposal even became more romantic when our partners got down on their knees and accepted our proposal.

We then handed them the gifts and hoped that they would like it. Akanksha slowly opened the gift. I could see tears roll down her eyes, when I asked her the reason she said "*Vipul don't ever leave me and go because you're the only one who I had loved after my mom and Dad*". I hugged her tightly and promised never to leave. The things which I gifted her were a box of chocolate in which each piece of chocolate was engraved with the three golden words '*I love you*' and the other one was a teddy. It's like girls die for those teddies and they have a separate place in their hearts for these teddies.

Nikhil gifted Nakshatra with a beautiful locket, a ring and obviously the last one has to be a teddy. It was time for our return gift. The return gift was quite surprising she pecked him on his cheeks.

It was lunch time and there were sumptuous meals cooked by Akanksha and Nakshatra. The food was lip-smacking and filled our tummies to the extent.

After lunch we ordered for some ice-cream.

It was around 5:00 in the evening by the time we completed our ice-cream. The date had come to an end. It was time for us to leave because Akanksha's dad was expected to arrive anytime. With a goodbye hug and kiss we left. I called up and told Akanksha just one thing "*Your return gift was too sweet. Can I get it daily?*" She replied "*Sssh, yes I can give you the gift daily, but only over the phone and with an ummh she cut the call*".

There are only two things which drove me crazy, the first one is the fragrance of her perfume and the second one is the smell of their hair after head-bath. Till date it remains an unsolved mystery as to which shampoo and perfume do they use which drives the people crazy.

This happens to me always, it's like whenever Akanksha and I hug; I completely get crazy with the smell. The brain stops working and everything around me starts moving on its own.

I left for home happily, but didn't know there was another surprise waiting for me. When I reached home dad called me to his room. After freshening up, I went to his room. He told me to come and sit beside him.

Then, calmly he fired the first question "*Who is the one with whom you talk late night?*" I replied "*Dad she's my friend*".

Now the second question was fired "*Is she your friend or girlfriend?*" I replied "*she's my girlfriend*" then was the third question "*What's her name?*" to which I replied "*Akanksha*".

It was time for the fourth question "*How was your day with her. Did you gift her something or not?*

Is it not valentine's day today?" I was completely taken aback by this question. I told him the complete story from where it started to the current day. He was quite impressed with my story and said "*If you ever need money or help do tell me*". I was like "*Yes dad sure*". When I asked him, why he was being so open today, to which he replied "*If you won't enjoy your life now, then when are you going to enjoy it*".

From then on, Dad was like a friend to me and I could share each and everything with him. I then called up Akanksha and told her about the conversation between me and my dad. She too was quite impressed with it.

The following day was the last day of our college, as the final examinations were about to begin. There was a small farewell party organized by the faculty. We spent some time with the faculty and promised to remain in contact with them. Those two years of life were filled with fun, memories. Within those two years, I found one idiot in my life, that asshole Nikhil, and the love of my life Akanksha. I got much more than expected in these 2 years. The farewell came to an end with hugs and tears of joy.

Now, it was time to get serious as the finals were on. Every one of us gave our best and hoped for the best. The exams went pretty well and before the results of our final exams, there were many other competitive exams lined up.

Those 2 months were the toughest of my life. The competitive exams included the likes of JEE MAINS, BITS, GITAM, SRM, VIT and many more. It was like only the books and we, upon that these 2 months went at a snail's pace.

The final examinations results were out, Nikhil and I had secured 85% and now the aggregate was around 90%. We were satisfied with the results. This satisfaction was not enough to celebrate as the competitive exams results were yet to be declared. These results were responsible in deciding our future.

Since, Akanksha was in medical stream, she had different competitive exams which were the toughest ones. The one fact that everyone needs to accept is there are only limited no. of medical seats with a huge no. of students fighting for it. The one who wins gets the seat. She was traveling the whole south to appear for these exams.

I was done with all the examinations and the results of these exams were pretty perfect. Now, it was time to choose the course and the college. Based on my Eamcet rank I was eligible to get a seat in CMG College of Engineering and Technology with the course of my choice. I opted for the course CSE which was purely based on computer languages. Nikhil too secured a seat in Geethanjali Engineering College with the course ECE.

Now, it was celebration time as each one of us had come out with flying colors and there was an occasion too, to celebrate. It was my birthday; I was just two days away from turning 17 and was pretty excited.

The day arrived when I officially turned 17. We partied hard and it was my lady love Akanksha who organized the whole thing. She was pretty adorable that day. We spent some quality time together before she left for Bangalore as her exam was scheduled the next day. I wished her the best as it was her last exam and promised me my gift on her return.

Nikhil and I went to drop her at the airport. I could see tears rolling down her eyes. I gave her a tight hug with a peck on her cheeks and then she left.

The next day I tried calling her but the only reply came from the other end was "*The number you are trying is not reachable*". I was a bit tensed, because this never happened before. That day I called her approximately 100 times but still the same message was read.

These incidents reminded me of the past. My heart started beating at a faster pace; the whole body had become bitter cold with the past incidents continuously rolling in my mind. I called upon Nikhil and told him the whole incident, he was shocked upon hearing all these things and said "*How could this happen?*" I asked him "*What happened?*"

His reply left me in a state of shock for a minute. He said "*Bro, just yesterday I spoke to Akanksha. She called me and said she had landed in Hyderabad and told me to pick her up, I thought she had told you. Upon reaching the airport when I couldn't spot you I asked her about your whereabouts, to which she said you were busy. I tried calling you many times and each time I called you the message beeped in as 'the person you're calling is busy', so without wasting any time I dropped her home*".

As soon as I ended the conversation with Nikhil a message popped in, it was Akanksha's message which read:

"*Baby, I loved you very much, but at present fulfilling my dad's dream is the first priority. He longs to see me as a doctor, so I thought temporary break-up would be the solution. We can get back into relation once I complete my MBBS Course. I got admission into one of the prestigious medical colleges in Bangalore, so before leaving to*

Bangalore, I am hosting a party and would love if you too attend the party. Please do come, Baby take care and all the best for your future".

When I didn't reply to the message, she called me and recited the same thing. I just cut the call saying "*it's your wish if you think break-up is the solution then let's break-up*". She then put up a message "*I know it's hurting you, but we need to break-up*".

I didn't respond to her calls nor replied to her messages. I tried hard not to cry, but these tears wouldn't listen to anyone. It's hurts when someone whom you deeply love just breaks off by saying my dad's dream is the first priority. I lost hope in everything and was in distress. Nikhil called me to check my health, when I didn't attend his calls he came running to my place. Seeing him, I could not stop crying, the pain, the love, the feelings, everything washed away in those tears. He hugged me tightly and said "*It happens, be strong*", but how could I be strong. This happened to me the second time.

The best natural medicine for your pain, stress, is your mom. If you ever come across this condition just go to your mom and place your head in her laps. She lovingly taps your head and sings a poem you like. When she taps your head with those loving hands, the pain just disappears. She has some god-gifted magic in her hands. The pain which I had was gone when she recited my favorite poem and tapped my head. I thanked god for giving me and everyone such a lovely gift i.e. a Mom. After getting relieved of the pain I dozed off.

The next morning Nikhil called me and inquired about my health. He then came to my place and reminded me of one such incident which happened a year ago. He said "*Bro, you remember the girl Madhu?*" I said yes, but what is related to her and this incident. He calmly replied "*A year ago, you were in relation with Madhu; our junior when I was seeing Nakshatra. She liked you when she saw you for the first time in the Exam hall and the very next day proposed you. I know you were not ready for the relationship, but still you accepted her proposal. Everything was going great between you both when suddenly one day you broke up with her stating that your first priority is your studies and most importantly the day you broke up with her was her birthday. She cried like hell and tried to explain you that being in a relation won't affect the studies, but you were adamant on your decision and the outcome was break-up. Still do you think this incident has nothing to do with the one which happened a year ago?*"

I remained silent for the next few minutes. He was right, I broke-up with her stating that my studies were the first priority and now Akanksha too broke-up with me stating her dad's dream as her first priority.

He reminded me of Karma. After this incident, I made a promise never to hurt anyone and this time I decided to enjoy my life without getting into any relationship because I badly needed a change.

Chapter 12: The Most Important Phase Of Life

* * *

I had experienced many relationships in my life, this time for a change I decided to enjoy my life with my idiots. This phase is the most important phase in one's life. It teaches you many lessons and also gives you tips of survival. It is the most memorable phase of one's life because you find some true idiots who will be there with you for the rest of your life. This phase of life is fun filled, with a box full of surprise and memories in it.

Finally, I was an engineering student. The kind of respect you get when you call yourself an engineering student is different because no one's bothered if you're an engineering student, as nowadays every household has one engineer student.

It was the first day of my college. The campus was a huge one with a large ground and a spacious canteen. We were directed to our respective classes. We had six subjects in our first semester with 2 labs. Every one of us was given the time-table and strictly instructed to follow the timetable. Since it was my first day, I didn't make any friends. The only thing every junior worried was the raging thing.

During, the recess hour there were around 3-4 lectures who were a part of anti-ragging squad. After the recess hour we were sent back to our classes since the senior's recess hour was about to begin. Every one of us was instructed to purchase the first-year kit only from the college stationery. The kit included items like drafter, chart box, textbooks, records, notebooks and various pencils used in drawing.

The classes ended at 3:40 PM so that we could get into the bus before the seniors could as their classes ended at about 4:00pm. The bus-in charge instructed the juniors to occupy the front seats as the back seats were meant for the seniors. We were told to follow their instructions else the student would get suspended.

The first day of the college ended with the introduction and instruction. I went home tired and fell asleep. From, the next day itself the classwork began. We were given loads of homework. The lectures threatened us with different punishments to get the homework done. Since, we were in the first year we had to obediently follow all the rules as the HOD of the first year was rumored to be strict.

The days passed by and by, now I had made quite some friends. Among them, was Raghu. He was from Maharashtra and I too, being a Marathi connected pretty well with him. We spoke of our life goals and also about our respective families. His family had settled in Nizamabad and he was living here in his uncle's house.

It was just two months since the classwork started when we were informed about the upcoming mid-examinations and were told to prepare well. This news made the students go crazy because none of us knew how the format of the paper would be. Just two weeks before the mid-examinations we were given the paper pattern. The mid-examinations were to be of 25 marks and assignments of 5 marks.

We prepared well and the question papers of these exams were quite easy. I had secured around 80% in the mid examinations while many of them even secured 99% in the mid exams. After the declaration of results there was shocking news coming our way, the parents-teacher meeting, which was scheduled to be conducted in the coming weekend.

Each and every parent was called up and told to come and personally meet the lectures to know their child's report card. I told my dad about it, to which he said "*Are they running a school or what?*" At first he refused to come, but when Mom insisted him to go and meet the lectures dad agreed to pay a visit to my college.

I took dad along with me and he met all my lectures personally and inquired about my performance in the class. That day I got to know why most of the parents opt to attend the parents-teacher meet because lunch would be served free of cost. I saw many parents even getting their siblings. At one point the whole family of a student got down from a mini tempo. They had brought the whole family, which consisted of about 25 members. I could hear the dad ask his son "*You get food today free of cost Na?*" His son nodded his head and the whole family went in.

Dad and I left after attending the parent-teacher meeting. On the way home, we had a sumptuous meal at my favorite restaurant '*The Chutneys*'. The food over there fills your tummy, but you still keep on licking your fingers.

I called Nikhil and inquired about his college.

His voice sounded very low, upon insisting he said "*Bro, Nakshatra and I broke up*", I asked him the reason for the breakup to which he said "*We are of different caste so, none of our family members would agree to our relation*". His answer left me stunned and there arose a question in my mind "*Does love need caste, do still people believe in caste system? Are we going towards development or going backward?*" But there was no one to answer my question because we lived in a society where still the caste system was followed.

I consoled him and said "*Move ahead in your life. If she's written in your life you will definitely get her and even the society can't separate you. So chill and enjoy your life*". He replied "*Jai bolo Vipul guru ki jai*" and we both broke into laughter.

After about 5 months into the college, we had the most interesting events. One was the traditional day and the next was the fresher's day. Both of these events were celebrated the same day. The event was scheduled on 31st December.

I wore a Sherwani and took another one with me as Raghu too wished to wear one. The whole college wore a different look. The girls were dressed in traditional attire. I guess some of them even tried to fit into their mom's sari. There were beauties all around the college and it was hard to control myself.

We then had songs which were particularly meant for the ladies, these songs were traditional ones related to Bhatukamma, a festival that is widely celebrated in the south. The ladies make a circle around a pot and clapped their hands.

All the lecturers and the girls started to do so. As we were hungry, we decided to have some stuff in our canteen. On our way to canteen an interesting thing happened. While we walked towards the canteen a set of seniors called us and asked us tell our BD. I didn't know what BD meant, so I directly asked them the full-form of BD to which they politely replied "*Beta BD means Bio-Data, chal abhi apna bio-data batha*". First I told my name, followed by the school name and then the inter college name. They were quite impressed by our answers and then left us saying "*Agar koi senior tumhe pareshan karey toh bolna Ravindra ka bhai hun*".

There was ragging going on in the canteen. The students were told to sing song, dance and tell their BD in different languages, but no one dared to rag us. We had some food and left. I was called to the sports room as the junior sports were scheduled to begin and I was participating in table tennis.

Gaurav and I were partners for the doubles. Gaurav was my classmate and a good friend of mine. He was an experienced player in table tennis. The first match was with a weak team, which we easily won. Then, after continuously winning two matches we headed to the semis. The opponent was a strong one; we had our strategy and went according to it. We were able to defeat them. Now, came the toughest phase the finals. Our opponents were far more experienced than us, but as everyone has a weak point they too had. There loop-hole was the spin, they couldn't play when the ball would spin.

The finals started. There were 5 sets of 21 points each. We lost the first 2 sets and then made a comeback by winning the next 2 sets. The last set was the game-decider. Everyone held their breath till the last point, but the game went into a tie. Both of the teams were just a point away from clinching the trophy. The heart beats increased, but we needed to remain calm and concentrate on the game which lasted for about 3 minutes and the last point when into our favor. We had won the doubles match of table tennis and the whole class turned to celebration mood. The whole CSE-B was overjoyed with the achievement.

Later, that evening the fresher's competition begun. It had three rounds: the first one was the ramp walk, the second one was to showcase your hidden talent and the third one was quiz round. The three rounds went brilliantly and the results were yet to come. Before the results were announced, the prize distribution ceremony took place. The winners of various sports were felicitated and prizes given away. When the anchor announced the winners of doubles table tennis, we went up the stage and there were students shouting "**CSE, CSE,** and **CSE**". It was a proud moment for us.

After the prize distribution ceremony, the results of the fresher's competition were announced. Both Mr. and Ms. Fresher were from our class. It was celebration time. Everyone shouted at the top of their voice "**Come-on DJ**". The music started and various filmy numbers were played. We tapped our feet's to these numbers.

By 7:00 PM, the DJ stopped playing songs as it was time for us to leave. The buses were arranged which would drop us home. I called on Nikhil and told him to be ready as it was party time. After reaching home, I showed the medals to my parents, who were overjoyed to see me with the medal. Dad came to me and asked "*Did you really win or did you buy the medal*". I replied "*Dad stop being sarcastic*". After freshening up, I left for Nikhil's place.

We partied till late night, when all of a sudden my phone buzzed and there was a notification which read "*One year anniversary with Akanksha*". I was like stop the shit we are now free birds.

With a soft drink in my hand, looking towards the sky, I recollected all the incidents of my life: right from my school life till present. Tears rolled down the cheeks, wiping them, I went up to Nikhil and said "*Bro, mere liye koi ladki dhund Na*" Saying this I dozed off in his arms.

The next morning when I reached home, I was welcomed by my family in a very different way. They were staring at me as if they didn't know me. Mom came to me and said "*Beta, go get ready, we have to go for brunch*". I got ready and then we went out for brunch.

The following days were the toughest ones as our semester exams were round the corner. By now, I had a group of friends. They were my second family. But, since exams were round the corner, most of them were not to be seen in the college campus.

The exams came and went in a whisk and then it was vacation time. The most boring part of the vacation is that every one of them goes to their respective hometowns and there's no one left to talk to. In the vacation days college seemed rather interesting. Only students with backlogs had to attend the exams.

Nikhil, Sandeep, Vishnu and I were the only ones left as our other friends had gone on a long trip. We went to the movies, did shopping and when nothing was left to do we slept. It was May month and the temperature soared somewhere around 45-47 degrees. It was tough to get out, so we decided to play indoor games, the best thing to have during this month is Sarjah. Sarjah, is basically a type of drink which is made from ice cold milk by adding bananas and Bournavita powder. All of these are put in a mixer and the outcome is Sarjah. It was our favorite spot during those days.

It was mid-summer and my birthday was just a week away. I had called upon all my friends for a treat. I was staying at my uncle's place with my two sisters and a brother, since dad, mom, uncle and aunt had gone out for a vacation. All four of us were having gala-time. Every day we used to cook different dishes. The best part was every night we used to watch a horror movie and then sleep with lights on. Whenever, any one of us had to go to washroom then we used to wake the other and tell him to wait till we were done.

It was 13th of May and I went to bed as usual. Later that night, I could hear whispers near my bed. I was afraid and started reciting Hanuman Chalisa. Someone called my name and since it was pitch dark I couldn't see anyone. Finally, with Hanuman Chalisa on I decided to follow the sounds.

At a certain point, I hit something very hard, it was the wall. I searched for the switches and when I found it, I switched on the lights. What I saw was surprising. My siblings were sitting on the sofa and were staring at the clock. When the clock stroke 12:00 they ran to me and then what, there was white cream all over my face. It was my birthday, I was lucky to have such lovely siblings. We laughed and partied the whole night.

The next morning it was my day. Raghu had come to pick me and then we headed to have breakfast. I had called upon all my friends for breakfast. After having a delicious breakfast, I was taken to a deserted place. Another cake was getting ready to be put across my face. I blew the candles and then all of them put my face into the cake.

Nikhil, Vishnu and Sandeep too joined the celebration. Later, after spending some gala time with my college-mates, I decided to leave for home. These three idiots came along with me to my place. Before I could get into home, there was another cake punched in my face. I said to them, "*You assholes never change*".

After the cake session, I went to take a bath. When I came out and looked at my phone and message popped in. It was Akanksha's which read "*Happy birthday to you Party Hard*". I went to Nikhil and said "*Bro, why does she message me when I don't mean anything to her*". He replied "*Leave her bro; at least don't spoil your mood today*". To which I said "*Party time*".

The vacations were about to end and now we were in the second year of our college. The college was scheduled to reopen within a fortnight. I looked for my books and my bag which was somewhere in the corner of my house. It took almost a week to find all my essential things.

Finally the day arrived when we were officially the seniors. It was our junior's time to get ragged. Before we could rag our juniors the results ragged us. My weird dream of having a backlog in my engineering was accomplished.

Yes, I had failed in one of my subjects and that one had to be advanced calculus. Everyone, including me, hated that subject; it was one of the toughest subjects you come across in your engineering life. Dad came to me and asked "*beta kya hua? result ayya?*" I shook my head and replied "*yes dad*" he then asked "*kya ayya result?*" to which I replied "*Dad ek subject gaya*" like others I too was afraid from inside fearing dad would scold me but something interesting happened.

He then said "*Beta I'm happy that you failed*"; I was a bit shocked as which parent would feel happy when their children fail. I asked him "*Are you not goanna scold me?*" to which he gave a mind-blowing reply, he said "*See one should fail in life because if you don't experience failures then you won't succeed. It is better that you failed now because you will learn from these failures. But yes, remember one thing you should not repeat this again*". Hearing this I muttered "*Bhagwan aise papa kisi ko na dey*".

Now, it was my mom's turn and as soon as I told her about my result, she turned towards dad and said "*Dekho appka beta fail hokar ayya hai*" to which dad replied "*Mujhe merey betey par naaz hai*". Hearing this mom turned towards me and said "*Jaa jakar padna shuru kar*" nodding my head, I left; because if I dared to utter a word in front of my mom at this situation then the whole place would turn into a battlefield.

She then turned towards my dad and said "*Aaap hi jaano apkey betey key baarey me*". I then vowed never to have a backlog in my life. Almost half of the members in my class had failed the dreaded AC exam and I was one among them.

It feels happy when half of the class is with you. If someone asks "*How many of you failed in the AC exam*" it feels proud to get up and say "*Me too*" as there is no point to feel sad when you have your friends with you.

In the 1st year I used to sit in the first bench hoping the lectures would be impressed, because it is said that the first two benches are occupied by the extraordinary students. Since I was no more extraordinary I shifted my base to the last second bench. I literally knew no one in the last bench.

Raghu had made 2-3 friends in the last bench and I had none. This is when I met two other idiots of my life, they were Pranay and Sanjay. Who knew these two would become my brothers from another mother.

In a less span of time I had found out my two idiots. We shared each and everything between ourselves. There was nothing kind of secret among us. Pranay was basically a Jain and he was the kind hearted among all, on the other end was Sanjay, was a mixture of Lucknowi, Bengali and Telugu, Raghu a Maharashtrian and me. We were like the Fantastic Four.

It was all of a sudden when one day Pranay Jain came up to us and said "*Bhai mera engagement fix hogaya hai. Tum sabko anna hai*". We were like "*Chal ja bey chutiya kisko banara*". He then showed us the invitation card. We were pretty excited as it was long since we attended a function and ate food free of cost. It was a weird thing for others because at a mere age of 19 years he was getting married, but he gave a damn shit to other's thoughts.

Since his engagement was just a week away, he took permission for leave from the college. The lecturers who were still single were envious of him and then what; the word of his engagement spread like a wildfire. Finally the day of his engagement arrived. We wore our best outfits and left for his engagement.

On entering the place we were astonished by the decoration. The whole hall was lit up by various colors. There was a plush sofa in the middle of the hall, which was for the couple; the specialty of this sofa was it would turn 360 degrees so that all the guests would get a better view of the engagement. In one corner of the hall, pleasant music was being played which comforted the guests.

There were various types of snacks which were offered to the guests. There was a place in the hall where all the items given by both the families were put for display. These included the ones ranging from electronics to jewelry. We tried on some of the snacks which turned to be delicious.

It was the couple's entry time. Everyone gathered to have a glimpse of them and we were busy trying out other snacks. There was a romantic song played during the couple's entry. Pranay wore a Sherwani and Trishla bhabhi had worn a golden color sari with heavy embroidery on it. They both looked elegant in their outfits. With hand in hand they moved towards the plush sofa which was waiting for them.

Once both of them were comfortably seated, the engagement ceremony began. Both of them exchanged rings and the best thing was while they were exchanging the rings the sofa moved 360 degrees so that each and every guest would get a better view. As soon as the ring ceremony got over we got onto the stage and congratulated them. I went to Pranay and whispered in his ears "*Bhai congratulations tere toh life set hogayi, agar bhabhi ki koi friend hai toh hamari bhi life set kardey*" saying this we both burst into laughter. We didn't want to take his much time so after handing over the gifts we left. It was now time to head to our favorite section, the Food section.

Upon entering the food section we couldn't resist ourselves. There was a wide spread of varieties across the table. Seeing these dishes our mouths started watering and before the water could overflow, we picked up the plates and started feeding ourselves. By the time we completed having our dinner it was almost 10:30 pm and as soon as we came out of the dinner hall every guest was giving us a weird look. We decided to ignore them and once we reached the washroom we got to know the reason of their weird looks.

Our clothes were spoilt; there were different types of colors on our shirts. I smelled them and it reminded me of the pasta. Our clothes had become a total mess. We had no other option but to wear upon our jackets and leave as soon as possible. We tried to avoid each and every beautiful girl coming towards us. Seeing us leave so early Pranay called upon us. He insisted us to come on the stage and have a photo session with him.

We told him to let us go, but he insisted and finally we agreed to get on to the stage for a photo. I had a beautiful girl standing beside me and as soon as the photo session started, the girl beside me asked me "*Do you brush?*" I replied '*Yes, I do*' and asked her why did she get such a doubt to which she replied "*No, I'm getting a strong smell of pasta from you*" I gave her a broad smile and said to myself "*How should I tell her it's not coming from my mouth but from the shirt*".

I decided to give her a witty reply and I started "*Do you bath?*" to which she replied "*Yes I obviously do*" and without wasting any further time I fired the second question "*Do you apply makeup?*" to which she again replied "*Yes I do*" and then she asked "*Why are you so bothered whether I put up a makeup or not?*" giving her a broad smile and getting one in return I replied "*It's because your makeup had spread all over the face and you are looking ugly*", I promise she wasn't, rather, she was looking much beautiful, but I had to do so and as soon as she heard this she stopped the photo session and went to her room.

I was relieved and said "*Phew, thank God she's gone. Now there's no one to smell my shirt*". After the photo session ended, we again congratulated both of them and were about to leave when she returned. Seeing her come towards me, I rushed towards the exit, she too tried to run behind me but couldn't succeed in catching me. I turned back and bid her goodbye and in return she showed me her red-blood face. With the help of signals I told her not to get angry else her makeup would get spoilt and as soon as I told her about the makeup she started to run. Bidding her goodbye, I ran towards the parking and said "*Pura kahye so hazam ho Gaya. Bhuk lag raha hai*" to which Raghu said "*Chal aur ek round ho jaye*" I replied "*Nahi bhai phir sey us ladki se panga Ni lena hai*". We then left for our home.

I was extremely tired that day and as soon as I reached home I dozed off. Now this whole lot of enjoyment was over and we were to concentrate on our upcoming exams. The one thing which I hated about my college was after every 2 months we had these assignments and mid-exams, the other best part of these exams were all the students were given the question papers in advance but still who has that much time to spend studying.

It was mid-October our vacation time, but our college management couldn't bear we enjoying our holidays so they put up the burden of writing records and observations. Once we were done with our observations there was another storm coming our way the lab internals and externals. The best thing of our college was we had no fests, or extra- curricular conducted in our college. After all these the parents are like "*Aaj office mey mera dost sweets baant raha tha*" and we would generally ask "*Oh uski shaddi hogi Na papa*" and our parents with a broad smile would reply "*Nahi beta uskey dost ke dost ke behen ka beta joh abhi 2nd year mey hai usko 90% marks aye*". After hearing this we wouldn't even dare to touch the sweet "*Kynki bhai self-respect ka sawaal hai*" and then we would say to ourselves "*Kabhi uno mereko mila toh usko chodunga nahi, usi ke wajah sey merey raat ki neend kaharab hori*".

The assignments went on smoothly. After the mid exams we all were given a surprise by Pranay. It was his marriage, he was lucky enough to get married so soon and we too were lucky enough to have a feast.

We did meet him in the college only once and that too, he had come to take the permission for the leave. The hot topic of our college had to be his marriage. He came to us and said "*Bhai plate dekhkar uthana ek plate ka cost 4999/- hai*" we burst out laughing and said "*U don't worry we'll get our tiffins*". It was finally that our brother from another mother was getting hitched. He called us to perform on his Sangeet but we couldn't because of these fucking exams.

The schedule was pretty interesting our semester exams were to start by the end of November and his marriage was scheduled just two days prior to our exams. We were in a do-or-die situation. Surely we didn't want to miss the marriage and were not even prepared for the examination. There is only one savior in these situations the supreme power the God. Basically, as the exams near, the faith in god deepens and the same thing happens with everyone. We were like "*Bhagwan yeh ek semester dekh Lena, bhai ki shaddi hai please".*

Now it was time for us to get busy, we were shopping as if it was our marriage and not his. I had ordered a gift from the vista print. The best part of this is you get to make your own gifts like your memories album or a photo of you on the tea cup and etc.

I was excited to attend his wedding; the venue of his marriage was Fort Grand. We never heard about this place before, so the next thing which we could was goggle it. In the photos provided by goggle it was pretty ok. There was a long discussion which went on from 2-3 days was that who all are coming, how we are going, at what time we shall leave, this generally happens when you have girls coming with you.

Finally, it was decided that I would be getting my car, then we would go and pick the girls and from there we would go to Kukatpally drop some of the extra weight from the car into the cab and then move on. Pranay texted and strictly ordered me to be there by around 6:00 PM. But as usual, everyone knows what might happen next when there are girls with you.

Sanjay, Raghu and I left at around 5:30 and reached the place where we were to pick our class girls. Then what, we waited and waited and waited. When the clock finally struck 7:00 the girls started to come one by one as if there was ramp going on. Noticing them comig I said, "*Hey you all are looking gorgeous, but why did you come so early?*" And a girl took my words seriously and went up to complete her makeup.

By the time we left to Kukatpally it was 8:00 PM. Thank God there were no girls in Kukatpally else I guess we would have reached the venue the next day. The next challenge was the destination; we didn't know where the venue was so we followed the maps.

We had to take a right but some asshole in our group said he knew the route and advised me to take a left and then we were going on, the only thing that was visible to our eyes was the beautiful moon and the road. The goggle was repeatedly saying "*You're going on the wrong route*" and that asshole was repeating " ". After driving for about half an hour when we gave up, the asshole said "*I guess we should have had followed the goggle maps*" and this asshole was none other than Sanjay.

After thrashing him left and right, we followed the maps. By the time we reached the venue the Baarat had already reached. We rushed inside and upon entering all of us were stunned by the decoration, the girls and everything. Fort Grand was a replica of palace, it was a wide spread area of about 100 acres. We were mesmerized by the beauty; it was basically a photogenic spot. The whole fort was lit up; a mandap was set up in the middle of the fort, there were drones continuously flying above us to capture the moments. It was like a dream wedding.

Without wasting any further time we started taking photos with every classmate of ours because these would be memories for us. After taking photos we greeted the couple and gave them the gifts. Pranay was busy that day so we didn't want to disturb him. We went ahead to food section.

This time there were many sections set up like the Italian, the south Indian, and the Chinese, etc. We vowed not to repeat the one that happened during the engagement. Starting with one section we went on to taste all the sections and when the sound of burp came out of our mouth we stopped.

After dinner the best thing that comes is dessert and who would want to miss a dessert organized by the Cream stone. I was busy eating when someone covered my shadow which was falling on the grass. Guess who it was?

It was the same girl whom I had troubled during the engagement. She was looking more gorgeous. The ice-cream along with me began to melt. As I opened my mouth to speak, she put a finger on my lips and gave a light peck on my cheeks. I couldn't control the animal inside me so in return I too gave her a peck. But before we could go any further I stepped back because the past incidents were flashing in my mind. I just ran as far as my legs could carry.

Later, that night she tried talking to me and I avoided her. What would I tell her? Will she believe me? Or would she again leave me and go? All these thoughts were rounding up in my mind. I just wanted to leave the place and go away, but it was my brother's marriage and I couldn't do so.

At around 3:00 am the Phera's started. We were a bit sleepy during the pheras and as soon as the marriage ceremony completed we left. It was around 5:00 am by the time I reached home. I was drained out of energy which made me doze off.

I could hear someone call out my name, rubbing my eyes I got up. It was dad who was calling me out. When I looked at the clock it was 6:00 pm. The first word that comes of every human when he has an exam tomorrow has to be "*Oh! Shit*". I started preparing for the examination and was confident that I would not clear the examination.

The next day I prayed to God and said "*Bhag-*

wan haam apkey bacchey hai thoda dekh lena". As soon as I reached college I was shocked to see the married asshole Pranay sitting and studying for the exam. Sitting beside him I asked "*Bhai exam key liye prepare hua?*" what a stupid question was it, how could someone prepare for exam the very next day of his marriage. He replied "*Bhai yeh doubts clear kar dey*" and we together solved some problems which were seemingly new to us, later to be joined by Raghu.

I went to the exam hall and seeing the question paper I was confident that I would fail. Once the exam got over my confidence level increased because there was no chance of me passing as I had attempted for only 16 marks and the passing marks was 24. Many of my friends came out dejected. There was a rule that all four of us would meet in the canteen after the exam.

Entering the canteen I could see smiling faces welcoming me. They knew I too was to join them in this subject. I went to Pranay and asked "*How was your exam?*" To which he replied "*Pakka fail*" then the same was asked to Sanjay and Raghu. Sanjay was pretty confident that he would pass and Raghu on the other hand was much sure about his failure.

The only talk going on in the campus was everyone asking for the subject notes because it would be helpful during the supply exams. There were 5 exams lined up and we cleared them one by one. Finally the exams were over and everyone's status changed to "*Mazee on, tension gone*".

As I already mentioned our college was a different one, every other college would get a month's vacation after the semester exams and our college would strive to even give us a week's leave, so we were left with no other option but to self-declare holidays.

During this self-declared vacation, I visited the most beautiful, calm place in south India, Murudeshwar. We planned the vacation with our cousins. It's a once in a lifetime, kind of place. The small city of Murudeshwar had a large statue of Lord Shiva which was near the Arabian Sea. We booked a hotel just beside the largest sea; the view from the sea-facing balcony was stunning. We stayed in that place for about a week. It was the memorable journey. There was nothing which we would get bored with.

After the short trip, when I returned home there were already rumors round the college that the results would be announced at 5:00 PM that evening, on the day of my arrival. I was a bit tensed and started surfing the college website and all of a sudden there was a notification, which read: *BTech 2nd year III semester results announced.* My hands began shaking while entering the hall ticket number. There was a white screen where the mark sheet was displayed, without caring for the marks I started looking for the grade section which was like PPPPPP, which meant I had passed all my subjects. I had even cleared the supply subject.

Till date it remains a mystery as to how I passed in the first subject. We four cleared all the subjects and were a kind of free birds now. The very next day, the classwork for 2-2 started. It was a tough time ahead for our new lectures to adjust with us. Our classes became more interesting because for almost all the periods only four of us were told to stand out of the class. There was a ma'am in our class who would love exposing her lingerie and as the saying goes there's a catch to everything. In this case too we had one such mate named Bravesh who entertained us in the dirtiest manner. He was basically from Punjab and had settled here because his dad's posting was in Hyderabad. His dad was an Army man.

The days passed by, and so did our semester. It just came and went in a whisk because you won't feel the time when you have some great assholes with you.

It was the last exam of our 2-2 semester and unfortunately the exam was Baap of all exams, the exam which everyone feared JAVA. If you hear the class and follow the lecture it's easy to clear, but I did the opposite, in almost every Java class either I used to sleep or would pretend to listen to the class. It is in the exam hall when those days flash back and you think "*Arrey agar us din class suntha toh aaj achey sey exam likhta*". Still, somehow we managed to fight back.

It was around 1:00pm by the time the exam got over and we had to rush, so we went to the car park, drove the car and reached home by 1:20PM. There, Nikhil and Vishnu showing off their 32 white teeth welcomed us. I parked the car, got fresh and booked 2 cabs as we were six members. The first cab was a sedan, so there was a stiff competition between us. Sanjay, Nikhil and I ran towards the cab and waving hands to our counterparts as we zoomed off and the other three assholes had to wait until their Indica arrived.

It was 3:00PM by the time we reached our destination i.e. Gachibowli. We started searching for the car which we had booked a week ago. Ok, I know you might get a little bit confused, so let me tell you the plan. Just two days prior to our last exam I came up with a plan, it was that we book a self-driven car from the Zoom car app and then drive it around the city, basically a night out. Now, the main issue was what we do until midnight, so I had a plan for that too. Logging into Bookmyshow app I came across something interesting, a horror movie, The Conjuring 2 which was about to release, so quickly I booked 6 tickets and we were done.

The reason to rush was, that the pick-up time of the car was 4:00PM. Finally, after about an hour of walk we located the place. Guess, what car it was, nah not a sedan but a luxury car, the Merck A class which every one of us dream to drive at least once in our life. Once we saw the car all of us were like "*Wow! Here comes the babe*".

The next big challenge was none of us had the experience of driving an automatic car. Raghu, Sanjay and Vishnu had already seen videos on how to drive an automatic car. So, Sanjay decided to give it a try. We hit the roads and as expected the car gave us shivers down the spine with it brakes and pick-up. All of us were hungry and the nearest spot was the Sardarji's Dhaba, what a place it is to eat, after reaching the place there was another surprise awaiting, the place was closed and it was scheduled to open by 5:00Pm and still we had half an hour.

So, one by one all of us gave a trial and learnt everything about the car. It was Sanjay's turn and when we told him to take reverse slowly, while he was taking reverse two ladies passed by him and gave an *'awe'* look at the car. I had no idea what happened to him and instead of applying brakes, he placed his foot on the accelerator, what then, the car's number plate slightly touched the wall, thank God there was no major damage. As soon as this incident happened, we shooed him away from the driver seat.

It was 5:00PM and we were the first customer to

enter. The aroma of the food was so delicious that only the smell could fill the stomach. Without taking any further risk of just filling our tummies with the smell we ordered for some food. The Chola Batura over there was the lip-smacking food.

Once we were completely filled, we left the place and yes only after paying the bill. We again hit the busy streets and went to Pranay's place. It was a dream come true for all of us because Pranay was not allowed to go for night outs, but this time somehow we managed to convince Uncle and Aunty and they too agreed on one condition that we visit their place before leaving. So, our next stop had to be Pranay's place. We freshened up, met Uncle and Aunty spoke to them and then after spending some time we left.

Now, the major confusion was where to have dinner? At first we thought Paradise and ended up with McDonalds. Suddenly, Vishnu looking at me said "*Bro, you've turned red, is all ok?*" I didn't know what he wanted to say, so I told that asshole to brief if and then he said "*Your eyes are full of blood red, I guess you didn't sleep the previous night*". Not only me, but all four of us had not slept properly the previous night. We didn't allow the sleep to spoil our enjoyment.

After having dinner, it was movie time and all of us were excited to watch a horror movie after a long time and it was Conjuring 2, its predecessor Conjuring 1 was too deadly. So, we expected this one to be the killer and yes, it turned out to be so. Once we got off the movie hall, the hairs all over the body were at 90 degrees, all of us were so horrified that we decided not to take the stairs, instead to wait for the lift.

As the lift arrived, we got in and to our surprise

there was couple kissing each other so passionately that I guess if the lift wouldn't stop the couple would have had a makeover in the lift itself. Getting into the car we zoomed off.

Now, the other question arose: Where should we head to? Sanjay came up with a weird idea. He told, let's go to Tivoli, all of us were like "*No bro, we don't want to lose our virginity*" because Tivoli is considered to be one of the red light areas in Hyderabad. After a tough discussion we come to a conclusion, that we would visit the place, but no one would get off the car.

We then headed towards Tivoli; on reaching Tivoli we could spot some Hirja coming out of a tunnel with a guy who was zipping his pant. Seeing them we were like "*Ekkk*". But Vishnu who was driving the car wanted to drive around the same place. At a point Sanjay and Vishnu were even ready to ask the rate. As our car moved closer, the Hijra started running in the direction of our car, closing all the windows I ordered Vishnu to just race away as we would lose away virginity to those Hijra's.

Ah! Finally, we managed to leave the place and vowed never to return. I guess Vishnu was desperate to lose his virginity after seeing the couples in the lift, hehehe. We then went to necklace road and had a photo shoot with the Merck babe. After the photo shoot ended it was my turn to get onto the hot seat. At first I hesitated and once I got used to it we zoomed off. What a car it is, we strolled here and there looking for new places.

I guess it was around 3:00AM when someone knocked on the car window. Wiping saliva I woke up and saw Vishnu beside me whose saliva was still oozing out of his mouth. It was Pranay at the window calling me out to ask what I would eat. I told him to get me an idly and by the time he arrived, again I dozed off.

By the time I woke up it was 6:00 in the morning and we were heading to the pick-up place where we were to return the car. After returning the car it was time to get back home, so we took a taxi and then dispersed with the memories intact.

After the vacations of 2-2 it was time for the third semester, now the gang of six had become inseparable. The 3-1 started and we were now known to be the last benchers or the duffers. The main goal of us was if one gets a punishment all the others do some or other mischief to get punished by the ma'am. Once Pranay got punished and then he looked at us and said "*Bhai akela khada hun bore marra*" so we three started laughing aloud and got punished by the ma'am.

We bunked almost all the classes and only attended a few, the best thing was we bunked the classes only to see the beautiful juniors. Sanjay was a kind of playboy. He flirted with every other girl and every other girl gave him a cheap look.

It was in the middle of 3-1 when Sanjay came to us and said "*Bhai ek junior mujhe pasand ayyi and I have her number*". When we checked his phone there was a funny conversation between the two, the message was like:

Sanjay: Don't get flat on my DP.

The girl: I'm not flat on your DP and stop being cheap.

It was the funniest conversation I came across; who says don't get flat on my DP when you hardly know the girl. He was of such kind. There was a shock wave sent to all of us, the creation of Section E. Section E was meant only for the toppers, but to get into the Section E all the students with an aggregate of over 65% had to appear for the examination.

On the scheduled day of exam, we four planned not to write the exam, instead we went ahead to watch the critically acclaimed movie Pink, which was a feminist movie. It was the best movie of all time.

Days passed on and the classes became boring. In almost every class we slept, sleep had become dearer to us. There were no interesting juniors to look at and no one to love. We had become lazy birds. It was during this lazy time, when I came up with an idea of starting a business. The first step was to set up this business in such a place where people would love to have one but don't. It had to be Nikhil's area i.e. Alwal.

Many students from Alwal com a long way to Suchitra just to have that one drink Sarjah. Sarjah was basically a drink which is made up with ice-cold milk along with a pinch of bournavita and a banana, the season of this drink was summer.

Since we were still in the mid of September, there was a long way to go. So, I started preparing blueprint of the profit and losses that might be incurred by the business and whether we would be able to bear the loss if incurred, the answer was yes; if our business would get into loss it would be minimal and if the business would get into profit then the profit earnings would be huge. Such was the business with a minimal loss and marginal profit.

The next big challenge was to find a proper place to set up this business. Nikhil had taken up the responsibility of finding us the place and he was given the deadline to find us the place by the end of the year.

Since, we were now in 3-1 it was the right time for the college management to put the placement fear into our brains. Every other day, the HOD of our department used to pay us a visit and tell us about the cut-off percentage and eligibility criteria.

Whenever the HOD used to start his speech, Pranay, Sanjay, Raghu and I used to joke like "*Sanjay tu Qualcomm ke bahar chai ka ek stall laga dey, Pranay evening ko chat ka stall lagata, mai raat ko bandi lagatu aur Raghu jakar order leta*", because we were confident that no company would hire us with a good package because four of us lacked that bookish knowledge, we didn't like to butty (rote) subjects but were forced to as there was no other choice left.

Butty reminds me to tell you all about one such student in our class who had done masters in mugging up the subjects. He is Sudhir, a good friend of mine, he used to mug up in such a way even the lecturers would go crazy. Like if there's a line for ex: printf ("it is a prime number"), he used to mug up this line by repeating it for almost 10 times. What a crazy guy he was!

The whole class was like a family to me, without them my life meant nothing: Msk, Sudhir, Kishore, Mayur, Ujwal and many more to mention were all a part of my life. The day would start and end with them. Among them was Vinay who like Bravesh was great at coding.

All of a sudden there was a notice circulated to the class regarding CRT classes, which were to be conducted on the condition of compromising our Dussehra holiday. There was an exam, which was conducted only for the namesake.

However, we were separated based on our aggregates. Pranay and Raghu were in batch-I and Sanjay and I in batch-II. At first everything seemed interesting, but later this whole lot was a piece of shit. We were bored to sit the whole day seriously and listen to the shitty lecturer.

So, to get rid of this, we made up a plan. The plan was simple we would bunk the class after the lunch break. After lunch break we jumped off the gate and went to the parking where my car was parked. Sanjay, Raghu and I were about to move when I spotted a guy coming towards our car, at first it was hard to recognize him, but when he came close to our car showing his 32 teeth's, it was then when I could recognize him it was our favorite asshole Vishnu. He too, accompanied us on our trip to Shamirpet.

We reached the place within 15 minutes because Vishnu couldn't bare the pain of being raced by a girl so he turned my car into a super car and overtook her. Upon reaching the place we packed our pockets with goodies, after walking a little bit there was the beautiful Shamirpet Lake in front of us. We took some selfies with it as that would be memories for us.

Looking for a shady place we sat under a tree which provided us the required shadow. The best thing was whenever we went to Shamirpet all of us would turn patriotic; we used to talk about the past wars and the present situation in Kashmir.

After spending some time and after some patriotic talks, it was time for us to leave for college, so we headed back with memories intact.

During the Dussehra vacations Raghu called me up and said "*Bro, let's have a barbecue night*" all of us gave a thumps up to this plan. We were pretty excited for the night, but before that something weird happened.

Both Raghu's and Sanjay's girlfriend dumped them for someone else, and both of them were teary-eyed. Seeing them cry, we three too started crying, helping them in that too, if our tears would dry up, we would take a glass of water and we would roll each drop down the cheeks. Very soon they came to know that we were being sarcastic and they too stopped crying. We could sympathize with Raghu but not with Sanjay because it was nothing new for him and the fact was that both cried for the same girl.

Finally, after the teary-session ended, we focused on the barbeque. With the Paneer, Capsicum and onions on the barbeque rods and below the grill was the red-hot coal, which was waiting for the barbeque rods to be placed on the grill. Once the rods were placed on the grill, the coal started doing its duty. After every 5 minutes we had to move the rods so that the veggies on the rods would get perfectly roasted.

Finally, our barbeque was ready. Sprinkling chat masala on the barbeque, we started to gorge ourselves over the food. Ah! The barbeque was splendid. At around 3:00 in the morning, taking our cars out we headed to Cream-stone: A place famous for its midnight ice-cream.

It was time to head home; by the time I reached home it was 6:00AM. I parked the car and headed upstairs only to jump onto the bed and doze off.

The days passed by and so did our exams. Within no time we were into placements. Each and every month, some or the other company would come and recruit the students with a minimal payee of 3.2L per annum. We were not recruited in the first round.

In the second round, however, there was a company whose eligibility criteria was 70% with practical knowledge. All four of us applied for the job, we went till the HR round. In the HR round there was just one question asked "*From you four whom should we recruit?*" We four looked at each other and were unable to decide. Pranay and I left the hall, now there were only two left Raghu and Sanjay. A few minutes later Sanjay followed suit.

Later, we three were called into the room. Raghu was smiling as he had the call-letter in his hands. Individually each one of us was interviewed. The question asked to us was "*Why did you leave the hall?*" And three gave the same answer like "*For us friendship means much more than job*".

We then asked HR, the reason for doing so. He answered "*See, if I would have had said this to someone else they would have fought for the job, letting their 4 years old friendship go, but you people didn't do so. I tested you in all the fields except the loyalty one and you four proved to be loyal towards each other. What more does a company require, when you have loyal employees.*"

All of us were delighted and congratulated each other. Four of us had the call-letter with a package of 6.2L per annum; the best thing was we four got placed in the same company.

It was now time for the other two idiots, Vishnu and Nikhil to get placed. I heard the same company which recruited us was visiting Nikhil's college too. So, I called him up and said to attend the interview. Nikhil and Vishnu both attended the interview; we were waiting outside their campus biting our nails. Both of them came out dejected, with their tucks out and heads down. We too were dejected and started moving towards the car parking, when suddenly a voice came from behind which was "*Bro's, taufa kabuul karo*" and showed their call-letters to us. We were like on cloud nine.

Everyone hugged each other and with joy of tears we partied hard. All the six idiots were recruited by the same company and the only thing that separated us was the blocks. Pranay, Raghu, Sanjay and I were in the same block and Nikhil and Vishnu in the adjacent block. Still who cares when you all are in the same company with different blocks?

It was party time and we partied till sunrise. Everyone from the class got placed with decent packages. So, it was convocation time.

Finally, all of us were given our degree and then what it was selfie time. We clicked many photos which would remain as memories since it was the last day of the college. Everyone hugged and with promises of meeting each other and remaining in touch, we left only to welcome a new phase of life which was waiting for us.

Chapter 13: A Twist In The Tale

* * *

It was the first day of our new life. We didn't want to get late on the first day. So, we left early in my car and reached office by 8:45AM. We were later called by our team leaders who gave us our first project.

Nikhil and Vishnu were in the adjacent block. We started working on the assigned project. The whole block was very large to be discovered and during lunch breaks, all of us six idiots used to meet and have a gala-time.

Whenever we had free time we went to discover the whole office block. During the project the one thing which we were addicted to was tea and coffee. Within no time, we made up many friends. A party organized by the company for freshers.

There were many seniors who attended the party. We had a great time interacting with most of our seniors. The main funda behind this was, we were told by each and every one that "*Always maintain a good rapport with you seniors*" and we did so.

The party went on well and it was around midnight by the time I reached home. Reaching home, I could see both mom and dad waiting for me. They were a bit worried and asked "*Itna late kyu hua*" to which I replied "*Papa office ki party thi toh thoda late hua*", staring at me sternly both of them asked "*Koi ladki toh nahi Na*", I convinced that it was nothing such.

The very next morning, we reached the office on time and submitted our project. Later in the evening, four of us were called by our senior and said he was impressed by our very first project and decided to give us a break.

Vishnu and Nikhil too applied for a leave and their leave application was accepted.

We were given 15 days off. So, we made up a plan of visiting Goa and then Delhi. Booking the tickets and packing the luggage we left for our first official self-sponsored trip. The only thing we were imagining was bottles and chicks. There was only one condition on which we moved ahead for the trip and the condition was: "*Not to lose virginity*".

Upon reaching Goa, the first thing we did was searched for a luxurious beach-side hotel, but to utter dismay all the hotels were booked. All of us were completely tired looking for the hotels, when suddenly Nikhil's phone buzzed and he was thanking someone over the phone. He came running towards us and said "*Bhai, hotel Ni mila but ek villa mil gaya*", we laughed and replied to him "*Bhai tu pagal ho Gaya Goa KO akkar, yaha rehney KO hotel nahi hai tu villa ka sapna dekhra*".

Grabbing his bag Nikhil started walking, we too followed him, hoping he wouldn't take us to some C-grade place. After walking for about 10 minutes, there was a large villa in front of us. He pulled the key out of a mat which was laid in front of the main door. Opening the door, he looked at us and said "*Is any coming in or are you staying somewhere".*

We rushed in and hugged that asshole who had arranged us a place to stay in. Now, it was time for us to discover the whole large villa, but before this we all wanted to know how he arranged for the villa. He started to tell the whole story, but let me tell you all in short "*He called up one of his friends who was staying in Goa and arranged for this".*

So, we started checking all rooms. There was one door to the balcony and the view from the balcony was stunning, the balcony was sea-faced which amazed us.

After unpacking all the goods, we were ready to visit the most famous place in Goa, the beach. The only reason people visit Goa is for the beaches and the pleasant weather. Getting into our shorts we headed for the beach. After spending some time at the beach, all of us were damn hungry, so we hunted for some vegetarian restaurants. When we couldn't find one, we decided to prepare food. Gathering all the essential ingredients we prepared some delicious meals which filled our stomach.

The next morning with a beautiful sunrise we headed to various tourist attractions and clicked some photographs. Evenings were mostly spent at the bench enjoying the sunset and later at night we prepared food.

The next day we headed to south Goa, where we finally tried our hands at the casino. Although we didn't win any huge amount, but still we did win in our first trial itself.

Returning to North Goa, we started packing our luggage because the very next day we had to leave for Delhi. Since, it was the last day in the Goa we decided to party. The clubs in Goa are a kind of different. There you don't get to see any person upset or stressed.

The party went on till midnight and we reached our villa by early morning. Freshening up and taking the luggage we boarded the train and dozed off. By the time we woke it was 7:00PM and then stretching ourselves, we got into some fun by shouting and singing songs. It did disturb few passengers, but later they too joined our madness.

Already six days of the 15 days got over and there were just nine days left. The next afternoon we arrived at the Delhi railway station. The one thing we did was we already had the hotel booked because we couldn't afford to take any risk.

Finally, we were in Delhi, our second holiday spot. Sanjay started looking for the beautiful girls around while we were busy unloading the luggage from the train. He was staring at a girl and she too stared at him, as soon as the unloading was done, we were ready to go when there was a person who was missing. Guess, I know you too might have guessed it right. It was Sanjay; we looked him here and there, when finally Vishnu spotted him talking to a girl.

We were looking around the station when all of a sudden Sanjay came huffing-puffing towards us and told us to run. None of us except Sanjay had the idea why were we running. Once we got out of the station we stopped and asked Sanjay "*Kyun itna bhagaya?*"

He replied "*Bhai mereko ek ladki pasand ayyi toh mai ussey baath karney gaya, at first we spoke well and then all of a sudden she changed her behavior and was like,' Chal rey chikney' and when I refused to go and ran from that place she too started running behind me*".

Phew! We were once again lucky, before it was

Vishnu and now Sanjay. We called up the person who promised to give us a car on rent. The car arrived and we zoomed away to the hotel. The staff at the hotel was quite extra-friendly and Sanjay on the other hand was extra-friendly towards them. We warned him not to create any further problems during our stay.

Once, we freshened up it was time for lunch, so we planned to order it in the room itself. After the delicious food, we planned to take a nap because all six of us were extremely tired by the journey. The next thing was to go around the city in the evening.

I woke up and went to the balcony as my quota of sleep was over. Rubbing my eyes, I opened the balcony door and then the only color visible to me was black. I was frightened at the thought that I went blind, I could see nothing but just black. I ran towards the bedroom and switched on the lights, everything was perfectly visible to me: The Television, the bed, Nikhil's legs and Pranay's shorts.

The next thing I did was checked my phone. The time read 1:30AM and the next thought that came to my mind was "*What the fuck, I had been sleeping from the past 12 hours*". I then jumped onto the bed which made everyone to jerk off. We then called Sanjay and Raghu, who were in the adjacent room for a midnight coffee and then we planned about the day.

There is a lot to see in Delhi, so we began with a trip to Red Fort. What a place it was, the most beautiful thing I have seen in my life till now. We posed for some shots and then headed to Agra to see the beautiful Taj Mahal, the symbol of love.

It was a straight two hour journey from Delhi to Agra. Upon reaching Agra we first visited the temple and then headed to Taj Mahal. All of us were completely stunned by its beauty. There was a fountain in front of the Taj Mahal. It looked even more beautiful than the pictures, which we used to see in the school textbooks.

The architecture, the carving and everything was made at such perfection that you just can't find any wrong in it. After spending close to two hours and clicking some memories, it was time to head back to Delhi. So, we bid adieu to the Symbol of Love: the Taj Mahal and started our journey back to Delhi.

On our way back to Delhi, Sanjay started praising the Taj and said "*I too would one day build something like this for the love of my life*" when all of a sudden I asked "*Which one?*" to which all of us had a hearty laugh because we knew it's not possible to build a large number of Taj Mahal's.

It was late in the evening by the time we reached Delhi, everyone was hungry, so we headed to the famous chat place in Delhi. The chat made over there is lip-smacking and as you tend to eat and eat without the knowledge that you have had enough.

So, we too tried the chat and yes, believe me it was as yummy as I had heard it to be. After popping on such delicious meal we tried the famous Kulfi in Delhi and it lived to our expectations.

We then headed back to our hotel with out-hanging tummies. As soon as all of us got in the lift, the lift too gave up on our weights. Two of them had to get out, so we threw Sanjay and Raghu out of the lift. Getting back to our respective rooms we dozed off in such a way that if anyone of us tends to move, then the other person would fall off the bed.

The next day was our last day of stay in Delhi, so we planned to do some shopping for the family members and then in the evening we would be visiting the India Gate. Once, we were done with shopping, we headed to the India Gate. This place is best to visit during the evenings when the climate is peaceful and during this time you get some picture perfect shots.

We saluted the martyrs of the 1999 Kargil war. It gives us the true Indian spirit when you salute the national heroes who sacrificed their lives for the country. It was time to get back and pack our luggage as we had to leave for Hyderabad the very next day.

Taking loads of memories with us we boarded the train to Hyderabad. It was a two-day journey from Delhi to Hyderabad. Although, it was not a long trip still we managed to cover almost all the places planned. Still, our bucket-list had many places to visit.

The two long days of the train journey back to Hyderabad were spent in a different way. We used to get up in the morning, eat and then sleep, later in the evening the same process continued.

Finally, we reached Hyderabad early in the morning. Unloading the luggage from the train was a tough task because while leaving, we just had one bag, but now every one of us had four full bags. I was helping Pranay with his luggage when a young lady knocked me off the train. Phew! The train was stationary.

There was blood rushing down my body and I was about to scold her, when I heard her saying "*Are you all right, did you hurt yourself*" and lent a helping hand towards me. I refused to take the hand and helped myself, but her voice reminded me of someone. I was like, '*I heard this voice somewhere*'. Cleaning the dust off my clothes, I started to search for her.

Pranay, Sanjay, Raghu, Vishnu, Nikhil and I started searching for her. Sanjay then found her walking to the exit and called us. We rushed and stopped her. I was shocked to see her, I was right, the voice was familiar. Even those five idiots were shocked and she too was shocked.

It was Sivangi, the love of my life. We met at the same place where we left some 10 years ago. I never imagined in my dream that I would ever meet her in my life, but as they say Karma. Yes, it is Karma, which played with us.

A single word couldn't come out of my mouth, I was speechless, and so was she and others. When we were finally back to the senses we hugged each other and tears rolled down the cheeks. I felt like the whole world had stopped and we were inseparable.

Heading to the coffee house, she told us how her family got to know about us and they sent her to Delhi to study and after about 10 years she was coming back to Hyderabad. She had completed her internship in AIIMS and taken a break, to visit her parents.

We were in the same train yet had no idea about each other. Both of us were in Delhi but neither of us crossed paths, but once we were in Hyderabad we met. I think Karma wanted this to happen. We met exactly at the same place where we bid adieu to each other 10 years ago.

I was happy to meet her and she promised not to leave me and go ever again. We exchanged our numbers and after a brief talk we both left. I still remember that day it was the turning point of my life because I never dreamt my life to give me such a twist, but this twist brought happiness back to my life.

We left for our respective places. I went home and distributed the goodies to my cousins. I brought a special gift to my bro-Vinit as he holds a very special place in my heart and then my parents, uncle and aunt. Everyone was delighted with the gifts and so was I.

After this I called Sivangi and asked her just one thing "*Will you marry me?*" There was complete silence for the next 5 minutes, only the sounds of traffic could be heard. I then said "*I know you might have got a doubt why did I ask you this*" still there was silence, I continued "*See, I am asking you this because I can't afford to lose you for the second time, life has given me a second chance which people rarely get and I am lucky to get one, so if you don't want to marry you can directly tell me no, if it's yes let me know*" saying this I hung up the phone and was nervously waiting to get her call.

Within 5 minutes the phone screen read: *Lucky Charm calling.* This brought a smile onto my face. I answered the call and said "*Thank you for calling, I was quite desperate to know your answer*" before I could say anything further, a voice came from the other end, it sounded masculine, the voice said "*This is Sivangi's dad here, it was me with whom you spoke, Sivangi is in the washroom and I know you.. You are Vipul if I am not wrong, the boy who was in relation with my daughter in her 10th standard*" this came as a shock to me, I was completely taken aback when I got to know that the person whom I had proposed was not Sivangi, but rather her dad.

Before I could say anything, her dad continued "*Vipul, I would look forward meeting you this weekend*". Nervously I replied "*Yes sir*" he then hung the call.

There was sweat all over my face. Apart from being her dad, he was an Army man and I know how strict and particular they are when it comes to their family. About an hour later, my phone buzzed, it was Sivangi's and to make sure it is her, I just said "*Hello*" and then the voice came from the other end as "*Oh! Hello why are you sounding frightened*" I narrated the whole thing to her and then what; she laughed the hell out of her.

She said "*So, Mr. Vipul are you coming this weekend or not?*" I replied "*Obviously yes, I want you and can do anything to get you*" by her voice I could figure out that she was blushing. After some romantic talk, I said "*Let's meet tomorrow and you tell me everything about your dad like his likes and dislikes, etc. etc...*" And then with a lovely kiss, I hung up.

The next thing I did was, I called up my five idiots and narrated them the whole thing and the only reply I got was "*Bachkey rehna bhaiyya bach ke rehna*". They promised to accompany me, but finally it would be me who has to face "The Army Man".

Chapter 14: Encounter With The Army Man

* * *

As decided the very next morning Sivangi and I met at a coffee shop. She described her dad completely from his likes to dislikes, his strict nature and his soft side. Now I had a detailed knowledge of my Father-In Law. Now, it was my turn to have some fun, so I asked Sivangi "*Do you seriously love me and you are serious about getting married to a flirt like me*" blushing she said "*Yes, I would love to marry a flirt like you*" and whenever she blushed her cheeks turned pinkish-red, that was the best thing of her.

We then spoke about our respective careers, about how to manage both personal and professional life because neither of us would be ok if both these life's crossed each other. We were speaking about this when all of a sudden my phone buzzed; it was a mail from my office. I opened the mail and read it. After reading the mail, I didn't know how to convey it to Sivangi.

Taking a deep breath I started "*Hey fatso, I just received a mail from the office and it says I have a six month project in the states, and I need to leave for the project by the start of the next year*". At first she remained silent, the face had shorn and the smile was lost.

She then said "*So baby, when are we going to marry. Are you sure of going?*" It was already March and there were just 9 months left for the year to end. Without any second thought I said "*Let's marry this year itself and the next year we'll enjoy our honeymoon in the states*" hearing this Sivangi replied in a naughty way "*So, is our honeymoon going to last for six months*" to which we had a hearty laugh.

The weekend was not far, I had loads of preparations to do so; taking a lovely peck on my cheek from the lady love I left and she went to the Gandhi Hospital where she had to perform a surgery. Rushing home, I went to Mom and Dad and narrated them the whole incident, they were quite happy with my decision of finally getting engaged.

It was 6:00AM in the morning, rubbing my eyes, I looked for my phone. There was a message which read: First Encounter with the Army Man. I said "*oh! Shit, it's Saturday and I have an appointment with the Army Man*".

Taking a quick shower, removing my clothes from the wardrobe a thought came to my mind, it was "*After marriage Sivangi would keep my clothes ready*" how romantic it would be. I was lost in the thoughts when Sivangi called me and said "*Hello Mr. Perfect I know you are dreaming about me removing your clothes from the wardrobe, if you want such romantic moment you need to first ask my hand, so get ready and please don't be late*".

Nodding my head, I replied "*Ok Ma'am command accepted*". I wore a black pant with a blue shirt and a jacket over it. The first thing that the Army Man liked was a perfect formal dress. Touching the feet of my parents and the lord I left in my car.

Everything was perfect, but there was nervousness on my face. So, now I started to pamper myself saying "*I can do it, he is just an Army Man*" but whenever the word Army Man would appear the pulse would start beating at a faster rate.

I reached the place, there was a large gate which opened with two army men saluting me and I replied them with a smile. There were seriously staring at me as if I had come asking for their daughter's hand. I drove and drove till I reached the parking area. Her house was a large one with a variety of guns hung all over the wall. I was guessing which gun would be used to sacrifice me.

I followed the servant's direction which made a way to the lawn where my meeting was to take place. There he was, my Father-In Law, oops the Army Man seated with a cup of tea. The beard, the dangerous look and the clothes spoke how strict and particular he was.

I greeted him by presenting the Army Man with a bouquet and a pen. The reason for the bouquet was that the Army Man was fond of red roses. With a smile on his face, he thanked me and offered a seat. He then told the servant something and sent him. The first thing that every Father-In Law asks his Son-In Law is "*How much do you earn*" but in this case it was totally different.

The first question I came across was "*So, by what time you get up in the morning?*" I replied "*Sir, I get up 4:30 in the morning*" without a single pause the next question was fired "*What do you getting up so early?*" to which I replied "*I go jogging and then some exercise*". He was pretty impressed with my answer, though I knew that I never wake until its 8:00 in the morning and about the jogging, let me tell you one thing, I never ever jogged in my life and exercise is a far thing.

But if I would have given him this answer then for sure I would be fired by the AK-47, so I gave him the answer which perfectly fit his question. He then asked me about my future plans and I told him about my business ideas and projects to which he was a lot impressed. I even told him about my trip to America. He was not pleased with it at first, but later when I explained him about the necessity and the importance of the project he gave a nod.

While we were busy talking, a hand came to me with a cup of tea. I looked up and it was Sivangi, she was looking adorable and the sari added even more beauty to it. I was completely lost in her beauty when suddenly a voice said "*Ahmm! The tea is hot, do drink it*" it was none other than the Army Man who now gave me a stern look and in return I gave him a smile because I didn't want to die in his hands.

Then after a brief talk the Army Man said "*Beta, Vipul see I have never ever brought a tear in either of my daughter's eyes and would hope the same from you, please do take care of her this is the only thing a dad can ask for*" this was the first time I saw a tear in my Army Man's eye.

I replied politely "*Yes, sir I would take care of your daughter and promise to live up to your expectations*". Hearing this Army Man replied "*Don't call me Sir, you can call me dad*" I was shocked hearing this.

Now, everything was fixed, only the elders had to meet and decide the Date of engagement and marriage. So, the very next day we arranged for a family get-together where both the families met and decided about the engagement and marriage. My sisters, uncle and aunt too were present for the get-together as we were a joint family and they always treated me as their son.

After lunch, as per our traditions a Pandit was called to study our birth timings and match them as per the traditions go. A date was zeroed in for the engagement and it was scheduled to take place in the month of May. No one had objection regarding the date of engagement, but now the main problem that arose was fixing the date of marriage because I had to leave early next year for 6 months and both the families, including Sivangi and I felt that if the marriage would take place this year itself it would be perfect.

Luckily, even the date of marriage was zeroed in and it was scheduled to take place on 19th of December. All of us were happy and satisfied with the dates and it was time for preparations.

Chapter 15: Everything Is Fixed

* * *

Now, everything was fixed and we had to do as per the schedule. I gave this news to those five assholes who were very much excited with the news of my engagement and marriage.

Finally, the holidays came to an end and it was time to get back to work. It was April already and I was a month away from getting engaged, the days were nearing and so was the work increasing day by day.

I used to meet the 5 idiots in the office and they would help me out with my projects. There was no time for shopping, so Sivangi had to do that one for me. I say she's perfect in choosing the clothes for me and I was lucky to have her.

Frankly speaking, I had no knowledge of the clothes to be worn but she was an expert in that. Pranay, Raghu and Nikhil would sometimes go home and help my parents with the arrangements; I guess without them nothing would have been possible.

Just a fortnight to my engagement I was sent to Europe to deal with a project. I was frustrated with the company, but a thought came to my mind which was: "*Business is business; there is no sympathy in business*".

I reached Europe and see how Karma played

with me, the schedule was that I would attend the meeting, give them a presentation and then once we were done with the deal I would return back, but something else happened. As soon as I reached Europe, I was taken to the hotel where I would be staying for the next 3 days.

The meeting was to take place on 5th of May but due to some reason the date was pushed to 7th of May, frustrated I called up my team head and he convinced me to attend the meeting. Now, it would mean that I would return just 2 days prior to my engagement. When this news reached home every one ordered me to leave the meeting and come back except one person Sivangi, she said "*Do attend the meeting and all the best! Come back safe*". Her words brought confidence in me.

The scheduled meeting went successfully and they were ready to do business with us. For this, the head of the office organized a success party and invited all of us. There was a surprise announcement to be made during the party. All of us were looking forward for the announcement.

The boss, got on the stage and everyone gathered for the announcement. He began "*Ladies and gentlemen, this party is organized to celebrate the successful collaboration with a top company, so let's raise a toast to the person because of whom the whole thing had been possible its Vipul, I would call him on the stage and yes the important announcement is that Vipul has been promoted and the next year he is going to America to work in the head branch over there*".

I took the stage just to say one thing "*This wouldn't be possible without my lady love*" saying this I looked at Sivangi and she replied "*Thank you baby that's so kind and sweet of you*".

We left early from the party because we were just 2 days from getting engaged and there was a lot of work to be done. The next day I tried on the Sherwani which Sivangi had brought for me. The Sherwani was light gold colored with heavy embroidery over it and the sharp Rajput shoes matched the looks, since we were Marathas there was a tradition to hold a sword in the hand and I too helped myself with the sword, when all of a sudden Sivangi entered and said *"Maharaj Vipul ki jai ho" to which I replied "Maharani Sivangi apka swagat hai"*.

The hall was decorated, lights were set up, sweets were purchased and invitations were sent and the last thing catering was done. We gave a rough estimate of 300 members for the caterers, so that there wouldn't be any mistakes.

The night before the engagement I was bit nervous and happy too, finally I was getting engaged to the girl of whom I dreamt. It was like a wish come true, Karma had lost and I had won this time. My five idiots were happy that I found my soul mate. Everything in my life was going great, no tensions, no problems.

That night I went to Sivangi's room and asked her "*Are you sure of getting engaged to me?*" She stared at me for the next five minutes and replied "*I would love to be with you till my last breath*". We bid adieu to each other with a promise of meeting tomorrow and this goodbye was incomplete without a kiss.

Finally, the day arrived. I couldn't believe that I was getting engaged to the one whom I loved till my last breath. All the guests had arrived and the Muhurat was of 8:30PM, I got ready and went to Sivangi's room. I waited for about 45 minutes for her and it was the day when I understood that girls really do take a long time to get ready, the waiting almost made me doze off.

Now, both of us were ready to rock. With hand in hand we headed to the stage where we were going to get engaged. There was some soft soothing music played at the time of entry, and a shower of red roses was made upon us.

We reached the place where the plush sofa was placed. Sitting on the sofa, it was now time to exchange the rings. I wanted to do something different so getting down on my knees I said "*Will you accept this ring, my lady love*" and blushing she replied "*Yes*" then what, I pushed the ring into one of her beautiful finger. The ring on her finger looked even more elegant.

Now, it was her turn, so she too decided something different. She got down on her knees and said "*I would put the ring into your finger if you promise to fulfill my wishes*" everyone was silent. I replied "*So, tell me what your wishes are?*" to which she replied "*My first wish is that you need to give me two kisses on the cheeks the one before you go to bed and the other one before you get off the bed. Now, the second wish is a romantic trip once a year, the third one is that on Sundays you have to cook for me and yes the last wish I want to get old with you*" before I could answer she continued "*So, if you're ready to fulfill my wishes I would allow you to place the ring into my finger*", all the people who attended the ceremony hooted and clapped.

I asked the guests "*Should I promise or let it go*" all of them answered in uniformity as "*Yes, accept it*", I looked towards her and said "*I think I would let you go*", pinching my leg she replied "*Mr. Vipul I am not going to leave you so easily*" and put the ring into my finger.

I gave a nod to her wishes and promised to fulfill her wishes.

Raghu, Sanjay, Nikhil and Vishnu were busy searching brides for themselves. After the gift- presentation it was photo session, everyone from the office attended the function including the chairman of the company. He congratulated me for the successful Europe tour and wished the best for my love life.

All of us were completely tired after the function. Sivangi and I dozed off, while Nikhil, Sanjay and Raghu were trying out their luck with Sivangi's colleagues.

The next morning was our first day of a new life. We woke up and the beautiful sunrise welcomed us with a smile. I had to rush to the office as it was my first day after the promotion, so fulfilling the wishes I left for office.

Nikhil and Sanjay had taken off as they had a date with Sivangi's colleagues. Only Pranay and I were present in the office that day, so the day got boring without them. It was lunch time and I had forgotten to keep my lunch. I was heading to the canteen to help myself with some food when all of a sudden my phone buzzed, it was a call from the reception lifting the call I asked her not to disturb me as I was on my way for lunch and hung up my phone.

I ordered for some Chinese, a few minutes later there was tiffin placed in front of me. I was damn hungry and upon that a tiffin placed in front of me, I looked up to scold the person and then to my shock it was Sivangi with a sari on and a tiffin on the table. I said "*Offo pati seva already started ah!*" She gave a cute smile and then we started eating the delicious home cooked food.

The days passed and so did the work increase as

I had to complete all the meetings and projects before heading to America. The plan was once I come back from America, we five would start our own business. It had been almost six months of our engagement. Everything changed like new technologies were introduced, the workload had increased, but the only thing that remained still was our love for each other.

I seriously feel there is some magic in love that keeps all of us together. It was mid-November and now it was time to book the hall, so the venue was decided as Novotel, it was one among the wedding places where you need to shell out money as water, but I believed in one policy "*Marriage is done once in life and who's going to take money with himself when he dies*".

Without a second thought, we booked the hotel for 3 days. The first day was the Sangeet, followed by the Haldi ceremony and then the third day Marriage. We selected the kind of design as wanted our marriage to be a unique and memorable one. The caterers were instructed with the menu and now it was time for card distribution. There were 15 days left for the marriage, so we went to each relative and distributed the card with a box of chocolates.

After the card distribution it was time for shopping. While going for shopping we were empty handed and once we were done with the shopping we had 22 bags full of dresses, now I leave it up to the readers to imagine how much pain I had gone through. Then the next thing was to visit the jewelry store. The fact about visiting this store is you go happily inside and once you are done, you come out thinking about how would you avoid visiting the place for the second time.

The next thing I would say it's very hard to get

such assholes in your life. They were like a family to me. Nikhil, Sanjay looked after the arrangements, Raghu and Vishnu were busy with the Caterers and I was busy lifting my love's shopping bags.

Everything was set the whole hotel was illuminated with different colors. There was a fountain erected at the entrance, red roses were hung up for the three day ceremony. With variants of light set up at the hotel brought the city back to life. I specially chose the hotel since it was in the heart of the city.

The day before the Sangeet Ceremony, I took my four idiots for shopping. At first like they showed off their shy part and then later they were ready to get going. It was a kind of men's day out, we shopped, cracked some adult uhmm jokes and then got back home in the evening.

Later, in the evening I personally went and checked if all the arrangements were done. I was not allowed to enter the Marriage room because there was something specially decorated for me and Sivangi and all this was done by those 4 idiots. All the families reached the hotel a day prior to the start of the Sangeet.

Both my elder and younger sister was happy with my decision about me marrying Sivangi because they were the only one who knew how deeply I loved her. I had something special for both my sisters and they were delighted to see the surprise, the surprise was a letter to both my sisters thanking them for the love and affection which they showed towards me and were always present by my side in both good and bad times.

The next morning, it was Sangeet, so an experienced DJ was called in to shake the floor. The Sangeet Ceremony was to take place in the evening, but the whole day went in a flash. It was around 6:00PM and the month being December the sunset would be early. So, around 6:30 in the evening the nature used to give us a feeling of late night.

The whole hotel was lit up because of which the city wore a different look. There were guests flowing in continuously, I was practicing my steps for the night. The DJ had already begun, one thing I could notice was no one looked sad or distressed every one of them was happy.

It was around 7:30 when we made our entry and were made to sit in a specially decorated chair. There were dance performed on some Bollywood beats, later there was a group dance performed by my friends and Sivangi's colleagues. Later both my dad and mom along with my Mother and Father-In Law danced to some old romantic hits.

Now, it was my turn. Getting onto the stage I told the DJ to play a romantic song and then Sivangi joined me in the latter half. The program ended on a sweet note. So, I decided to give her a surprise. I sang a song which brought a together, let me give us a chance to guess, you all might have gone across it. The song that brought us together and it was none other than "*Sun Raha hai na tu*" the song which was playing during our first weird meet.

After the Sangeet it was time to gorge onto some delicious food. The aroma was very strong which attracted a number of guests towards the food zone. We had our dinner by 11:30, the food was extremely delicious and it was above expectations.

At around midnight after everyone had their dinner, it was time to doze off because the next day was the Hadli Ceremony and it is one of the most important and religious ceremonies in one's life. Sivangi and I were not allowed to sleep on the same bed because it was considered inauspicious to sleep together before marriage. I was not that kind of person who believed in all this, but Sivangi had a strong belief in this. So, for her sake I decided to sleep in a separate room. Within 5 minutes of getting into the bed, I dozed off.

"It was the day of my marriage everyone was happy; Sivangi was looking stupendous in her bridal dress which consisted of a gold-color embroidered sari, the matching earrings, the bindi on her forehead and a small but elegant necklace around her neck made her the most beautiful bride in the whole world. The cute smile of hers could kill thousands of men around her, all of a sudden the whole happy atmosphere turns gloomy and a sad one. There is silence everywhere, I was unable to figure out what had happened, when suddenly someone started pulling me away from the place where I was to actually sit and get married with the love of my life, I started shouting and calling out everyone, but there was no response, the people around me were like statues, no one could hear my cry, I screamed 'Sivangi, Sivangi' but she too did not respond. She stared at the entrance as if she was waiting for someone to arrive, I guess it was me but I had arrived a long time ago, then whom was she looking out for? I called my four idiots but they too were staring at the entrance with tears in their eyes, I couldn't move the hand that was catching me so strong, it was impossible to free myself from his clutch, the whole place which was full of life turned like a place of silence, the one question went unanswered was why were all of them looking at the door when I had already arrived, whom were they searching

for and who was the person who held me so tightly and dragged me away" before I could see anything further the alarm rang and the sound was so strong that I almost fell off the bed.

Taking deep breaths I rushed to see Sivangi. She was preparing tea and some snacks for the family members. Seeing her I was relieved, but the dream, what was it what did it want to convey, what happened next were the questions that were surrounding me and I had no answer to it. I went to Sivangi and hugged her tightly. She placed a sweet but naughty kiss on my cheeks and I too gave one in return not on the cheeks but on the forehead.

I went to my elder sister and told her about this weird dream. She laughed and said "*Bro, it's nothing just a dream don't think about it much because you are already stressed, why don't you go and have a massage you will feel relaxed and yes get ready it's Haldi today, you are just left with 24 hours so enjoy as much as you want*" saying this she left because she had a lots of work to do.

I wanted to tell Sivangi about this dream, but then a thought came to my mind that, it makes no sense by giving her trouble. So, I let it go and went to have a massage. Seriously, massages do give you a relax and fresh feeling. After the massage session I took a steam bath which relaxed both mind and body.

It was time for Haldi ceremony. The tradition is that first Haldi is put all over the body of bride and then the same Haldi is sent to the groom and a part of groom's Haldi is sent to the bride who applies it on the body and vice-versa.

One by one each of my relatives put Haldi on my body. It was now the four idiots turn to put Haldi over my body. They not only put Haldi over my body, but smashed my face into the bowl of Haldi.

After everyone applied Haldi, it was time to take bath. After taking a hot steam bath, I went to sleep. It was around 4:00 in the evening when my sleep broke with the sound of arrangements which were taking place just beside the room in which I was sleeping. Then I had to rush to see if everything was in place for the big day, which was just 15 hours away. Everyone present there was looking happy and looking forward for the big day.

It was late in the evening when Sivangi and I decided to have a romantic time just before the big day. So, we sneaked out to spend some time with each other. I played a romantic song, with hand in hand, we looked into each other's eyes, there was love in the air. After the romantic dance I organized for a candle light-dinner in the lawn where no one would come.

During the dinner, Sivangi said "*Baby, I consider myself lucky to get you and today I make a promise to be with you in your bad and good times, but you promise me one thing you will never leave me and go*". I replied "*I promise you I will never ever leave you till my last breath and even later*" to which she got emotional, and her inner beauty that was oozing out could be seen on her face.

Soon, after the dinner we left for our respective rooms. I went and had a last minute check to all the arrangements except the function hall because there was something special waiting for both of us.

It was around midnight when I got a call, the phone rang 2-3 times but I ignored it. When the phone refused to stop I picked the call, it was my boss at the other end, he said "*Vipul, sorry to disturb you, but if pos-*

sible can you come and meet me, I want you to complete all the formalities before leaving for America".

I replied "*Sir, can I come and do this work later, after my marriage*" to which the boss replied "*I would also not want to disturb you but I am leaving for America and I would be returning next year so I would like you to come and complete all the formalities*"

I replied "*Ok, sir, I will be there within 30 minutes*" and hung the call. I went to tell Sivangi that I would be leaving for some office work. So, I headed to her room upon opening the door, I saw that she had already slept, so without disturbing her I went into her room and placed a kiss on her forehead.

All the four idiots were too asleep. I decided to leave and return as soon as possible. With clothes on, taking the car I left.....

Chapter 16: The Untold Tale

* * *

I guess there is no introduction needed for us *'right'*. We are the four idiots, which Vipul always used to refer to. It was Vipul's dream to complete his story and we are the ones who are going to tell you the untold and unheard tale.

I am Nikhil who's writing the part with the help of Vishnu, Sanjay and Pranay. It was around 3:00AM in the morning when my phone buzzed, it was from Vipul, I answered the call and asked him "*Where are you?*" to which he replied "*I am at my office, came out to complete all the formalities before leaving for America*" he continued "*I am very excited bro, finally I am getting married, I know every one might be in deep sleep so I called you up, guess what, I spoke to Nakshatra's parents and they have agreed to marry her with you, now only Vishnu, Sanjay and Raghu are left and yes I have another news for you idiots, you all are coming to America in the month of February. I have spoken to our boss and he agreed for your transfers, we'll have too much fun over there*".

I replied "*Vipul come early don't get late, we'll be waiting*" before I hung up the phone, he said "*Give my love to Sivangi, tell her I'll be back soon*".

It was around 5:00 in the morning, everyone was awake and preparations were in full swing for the big day which had finally arrived. Vipul was eagerly waiting for this day and all of us were happy for him.

We got busy looking after the arrangements and the first thing we did was called the professionals and decorated the hall, the background was decided to be photos of the couple. So, we brought in the projector and did a trial. Everything was perfect, the background contained the photos of Vipul and Sivangi and every second there were memories that flashed up in the background, the happy moments which they spent together.

The next task was to decorate the couple's bedroom. We left no stone untouched in the preparations. Now, it was time to go and check if Vipul was ready or not. We knocked his room, but there was no response, we thought that he would be tired and might have dozed off, so we decided to let him sleep for some time.

I went and checked for Vipul's car as I needed to decorate it, but couldn't find his car. So, I informed Vishnu and Sanjay about it, they too started checking for his. When we could find we rushed to his room with a duplicate key, to our shock there was no one in the room. A number of thoughts ran in my mind. *Where was he? Did he run away? Was he fine? If he is in some trouble then why didn't he call us?*

We searched the hotel thoroughly, but there was no clue about him. At one point, we decided to go and tell Sivangi about Vipul's absence, but later a thought came to the mind that it would not be right to worry her as it was her big day.

So, we decided to split up and search for our brother who was missing. I, Sanjay and Pranay called up his colleagues and asked about him, Raghu and Vishnu looked for him. Later, when everyone said they didn't know about him, we directly called the boss who was about to leave for America.

I asked the boss about Vipul's whereabouts to which he said "*Vipul had left the office at around 3:00 in the morning and was very excited about his trip to America*" I recollected "*Yes, Vipul had called me at around 4:00 in the morning and said he was coming home*"

His disappearance was a mystery to all of us. We tried our best, but couldn't trace him. It was about 4:00 in the evening and all the guests had arrived to wish the couple the best. Sivangi, too was getting ready for the big evening.

But, we were still searching for our missing brother. I guess it was around 4:30 in the evening when my phone buzzed and the unexpected happened. Getting into the car we rushed to the place where we were called. The caller sad that he had found Vipul, there were tears of joy and we were happy to find him.

Upon reaching the place, we saw a large crowd surrounding the spot. At first we were surprised to see such a large crowd, but when we got to the place, the thing we saw sent shivers down the spine. Vipul's car was overturned and his body lay in a pool of blood. Just about 10 minutes ago we were happy to find that asshole, but never imagined that we would meet him in this way.

None of us was able to move, there was complete silence, tears rolled down the cheeks. Our best friend, a brother, happy going person lay dead in front of us. We knew how excited he was about his marriage. He dreamt large and he was the most emotional person amongst us, he was full of life and never prayed for anyone's bad. Today, he lay dead in front of us. *How could*

God take such a person who was full of life and always wanted to see people around him happy... What was his fault? There were many questions in the mind, but there was no answer.

The police arrived at the spot and took a survey of the place. Now, the difficult task was how we would tell this to Sivangi who was equally happy as him. The whole way back to the hotel, my phone kept on ringing it was Sivangi who was calling. I didn't have the dare to answer the call and tell her what had happened.

So, we decided to go back and tell her. On reaching the hotel we saw Sivangi who was in her bridal dress waiting for us. The first question she asked was "*Where is Vipul? Didn't he come with you, I know he hasn't come back since morning and you were telling that you found him, where is he. Why isn't any one of you answering? Is he all right no, c'mon tell, speak up?*"

We couldn't utter a single word, nor could answer her question. She understood the answer, as our silence was her answer. She then asked "*What happened, tell me?*" to which I replied "*Sivangi, Vipul is no more among us. He died and the reason is not known, his body lay in a pool of bed when we went to see it. The police had taken the body for post-mortem, and we are expecting to know the reason at the earliest. Listen, Vipul always loved you and his love for you will remain eternal*".

Hearing this entire thing, she just said "*I want my husband's body back. I don't want it to be cut into pieces just in the name of post-mortem. Just do me one favor please get me my husband's body right now*".

Just then Vipul's elder sister came and told us about his dream. It was similar to the whole incident. All of us were looking at the entrance, hoping Vipul would arrive, but the truth was he would never. Sivangi, refused to listen to anyone.

What more could Sivangi ask for, she was completely broken by this thing. They both were the happiest couple I had ever seen and both of them were pretty excited for this day, but just an hour before the marriage destiny had some other plans for them.

We rushed to the police station and refused to perform postmortem on our brother's body. There was another shocking news coming our way, the police had caught the driver of the truck because of whom our brother was no more.

After interrogation, the driver gave a statement saying that he was drunk and didn't notice Vipul's car coming from the other end. The truck driver was driving in the wrong lane and Vipul had even warned him by showing dipper, but he was heavily drunk that he didn't slow rather hit Vipul's car which overturned and Vipul died on the spot itself.

Taking the body we went to the Hotel, Sivangi was still waiting to see her husband's body. What was the fault of her; because of such drunken driver many lose their loved ones.

Seeing Vipul's body Sivangi fell unconscious, later when she gained consciousness, she kept on staring at Vipul's body, tears rolled down the cheek. The whole place which was 2 days ago full of life now turned as a place of sorrow and grief. The place had become lifeless with tears in eyes and pain in heart. We now had only memories of him, but not him.

Many people thronged to pay him a last visit. The next day, his body was taken to the burial ground and with all the rituals and traditions; his body was burnt on a pile of wood. Collecting the ashes, we headed to Ganga where his ashes were let into the water.

There were many questions that were unanswered like: *How can God be so cruel? Is this Karma for which he payed the price? Was the dream real? Are people going to lose their dear ones because of the fault of others? When is the government going to take action against such people who drink and drive?*

But one Person who did not lose hope was; his love Sivangi. Every year she visits the railway station and waits for the Delhi Express to arrive, we too, accompany her and then when everyone gets down she goes to each compartment and searches for Vipul hoping for a miracle that one day he might come back into her life.

There was no chance for any miracle, life had given him everything and in return took away only one thing, his life which was valuable.

He did leave us and go, but always remained in our memories. I still remember the day when he first met her and his whole life story flashes in front of me whenever I think about him. With tears in eyes, rolling down the cheeks every year we light candles in the same Hotel and every beggar is given a pair of new clothes because Vipul always loved to help the poor. We couldn't get our brother back, but in return we could fulfill his dreams.

He is the one who taught us the way of living life and today he wasn't with us. He always told the right thing which will always remain in our mind "Live life not to just earn and die, have some good memories so that people will remember you lifelong".

The only thing which she had was the locket which he had gifted her and told her to open only when he was no more. She opened the locket and there was a small let-

ter with a cute picture of them. Upon opening the letter, tears rolled down her eyes, it was written "I know that you might open the letter only when I am no more. There's only one dream of mine; to love you till the last breath and if possible, even after that. I want to get old with you and spend the rest of my life just looking at the memories which we spent together".

The other thing that surprises us is we still feel that Vipul is present somewhere around us and is keenly watching his four idiots making his dream come true. Within years, our company which was named as "Brothers for Life" was one of the leading companies in the world and whatever we got for our achievements were dedicated to our beloved brother Vipul who will always remain in our Memories.

.

From the glimpse of darkness to the ray of sun, there you get laid in the grave which you dig it for others.

What goes around comes around. Mark my name peeps

*It's **"KARMA"** the beloved witch*

So, to know who I am turn around the book and start reading.

For feedback: vipulbarpute3@gmail.com

About the Author

* * *

Vipul Barpute along with his friends reminds us the moment of every man's first walk with innocence - the school, the second phase where we walk through our dreams - intermediate and the third phase which helped in achieving our goals and the one we are going to miss the most in our life - Bewitch karma is the word that takes care of our life if we are not going to take care of it. So he knew the mistakes which he had done are taken care by his dearest love "karma" to know his mistakes and the actions of karma and to know where he is now,the answer is here "KARMA ,THE BEWILDERED WITCH".

www.ing
Lightning
Chamber
CBHW02
48282C